JOB

JOB

GOD'S SOVEREIGNTY
IN SUFFERING

RONALD HANKO

REFORMED
FREE PUBLISHING
ASSOCIATION
Jenison, Michigan

Reformed Free Publishing Association
1894 Georgetown Center Drive
Jenison MI 49428
616-457-5970
www.rfpa.org
mail@rfpa.org

Cover design by Erika Kiel
Interior design by Katherine Lloyd / theDESKonline.com

ISBN: 978-1-944555-82-5
ISBN: 978-1-944555-83-2 (ebook)
LCCN: 2021933524

Dedicated to
all God's suffering saints

CONTENTS

Part Four: The Third Round of Speeches

Part Five: Elihu's Entry

Part Six: God and Job

PREFACE

—

There have been many words written on what C. S. Lewis called "the problem of pain,"[1] the relationship between God and suffering. The answers to this problem, if indeed it is a problem, have also been many. Some use the existence of suffering to deny the existence of God. Others deny that God is in any way the originator of human suffering. Still others speak of a paradox.

The book of Job is different. Though it consists largely of speeches by Job and his friends, it is not a human response to suffering endured or observed. The book of Job is God's own word concerning pain and suffering, especially the suffering of his people. This commentary will proceed, therefore, from the perspective that the book is inspired and infallible, given to us by God's Spirit as an explanation of our own suffering and the suffering we witness.

To say that the book of Job is inspired and infallible is not to say that every word spoken by Job, by his friends, and by Satan is truth. Many things said in the book are wrong either in their content or in their application, but that is often the case in scripture. Nevertheless, the content of the book is the Holy Spirit's infallible account of the interaction between Job and his friends as they contemplate suffering on a scale seldom seen. More, it is God's final word on the matter.

---

1   C. S. Lewis, *The Problem of Pain* (London: The Centenary Press, 1940).

Nor is the poetic nature of the book of Job an objection to its inspiration and historicity. Either the characters in the book actually did speak in poetry—something not so strange, given the nature of Hebrew poetry—or the Holy Spirit in inspiring the book turned it into poetry. It would be difficult to imagine someone speaking in English poetry, since our poetry is very different with its meter and rhyme, but poetry in the Bible consists of parallel statements that say the same thing, more or less, or even say the opposite, thus explaining and expanding on each other. It is not so difficult to imagine people speaking in that manner. In any case, the poetic nature of the book only makes it more memorable and instructive.

This commentary also assumes that Job was a real historical figure. He is mentioned with other historical figures, Noah and Daniel, in Ezekiel 14:14, 20, and James assumes his historicity in James 5:11. The book of Job is not a parable or allegory or a retelling of ancient legends that have a universal message or moral to them. Though the events recorded in the book—Job's loss of everything, the appearances of Satan in heaven, God's appearance to Job in a whirlwind, and the restoration of Job's fortunes—are unusual, they are no more unusual than the rest of scripture and not unusual at all to one who believes in a sovereign and every-where present God.

Through the suffering of Job, God speaks to all of us concerning our trials and the suffering that is so much a part of life. God's message is summed up in James 5:10–11: "Take, my brethren, the prophets, who have spoken in the name of the Lord, for an example of suffering affliction, and of patience. Behold, we count them happy which endure. Ye have heard of the patience of Job, and have seen the end of the Lord; that the Lord is very pitiful, and of tender mercy."

This commentary will not be a verse by verse explanation of Job. That would require too much space, would almost certainly be repetitious, and would obscure the main purpose of the book. This commentary shows how the book fits together and how the different speeches develop and build on one another. For that reason this commentary owes a great deal to the recently republished and long unavailable *The Argument of the Book of Job Unfolded*.[2] Though I do not agree with some of that book's theology, it was most helpful in seeing the overall pattern of the book.

May God bless what is written here and use it for the comfort of his people until every tear is wiped away and there is no more sorrow or suffering. May he use the book to turn us to him who was touched with the feeling of our infirmities and who is able to help those who suffer. May the Redeemer whose coming and glory Job saw be our only comfort in life and in death.

---

2   William Henry Green, *The Argument of the Book of Job Unfolded* (New York: Robert Carter and Bros., 1874). Republished as *Conflict and Triumph: The Argument of the Book of Job Unfolded* (Edinburgh: Banner of Truth Trust, 1999).

Part One

THE HISTORY
OF JOB

1

INTRODUCTION

The author of the book of Job is unknown. Jewish tradition ascribes the book to Moses; other suggestions are Job himself or Job's friend Elihu, who comes on the scene in chapter 32. The Spirit has not seen fit to tell us who the human author is, and the question of human authorship is unimportant. The real author is the Holy Spirit, and the book is part of the inspired word of God. This is God's own word concerning our suffering.

The place of Job in the word of God has never been questioned. If there were any doubts, they should be laid to rest by the reference to Job in James 5:10–11. When James says, "Ye have heard of the patience of Job," he as much as tells us that Job belongs in the word of God and assumes that the believers to whom he is writing have heard of Job and his struggles and of God's mercy to Job.

Both James 5:10–11 and Ezekiel 14:14, 20 establish the inspiration of the book as well as the historicity of Job. In both, Job is viewed as an historical person and as an example of believers. The book of Job is also quoted once in the New Testament: Paul quotes Job 5:13 in 1 Corinthians 3:19, when he writes, "He taketh the wise in their own craftiness." There Paul uses the phrase, "It is written," a phrase that always refers to other portions of the word of God.

In the Hebrew Old Testament Job is part of what are called the Writings, and it is usually placed after Proverbs and before Ecclesiastes. The Protestant tradition of placing the book before Psalms traces back to the Latin Vulgate. Since, however, the order of the books of the Bible is not inspired, it makes no real difference where the book is placed and in what order it is read with the other books of the Bible.

Some date the book of Job to the return from the Babylonian captivity, but there are a number of clues, including the language of the book, suggesting that it is very early, perhaps the earliest book of the Bible. Even more certain is that Job himself lived around the time of the patriarchs (1800–1700 BC) and was a near-contemporary of Abraham, perhaps one of those whom Abraham left behind when he migrated to Canaan.

There are other clues as well to the early date of the book. There are no references in the book to Israel or to Israel's history, suggesting that it predates the rise of that nation. Most agree that the land of Uz, Job's homeland, was in northern Arabia or further east, between Damascus and the Euphrates. If this God-fearing man was from that area, he must have lived prior to disappearance of the knowledge of God there, around the time of the patriarchs or shortly after. The offering of sacrifices by Job as head of his family also suggests a time prior to the establishment of the Mosaic priesthood, and the age at which he died (Job 42:16) would put him in the post-Babel era, around the time of the patriarchs.

It is possible that the land of Uz is in the area of Edom. Lamentations 4:21 makes reference to the "daughter of Edom, that dwellest in the land of Uz," and there was an Uz who was a descendant of Esau (Gen. 36:28). That would place Job later in history, around the time of Jacob, and Job would have lived to the south-east of the land of Canaan, but the book would still date to the time of the patriarchs.

The best clue, however, is the reference to Elihu the Buzite, the kinsman of Ram, in Job 32:2. If, as many believe, the Buzites were near neighbors of the Chaldeans, if Buz is the same person as the man mentioned in Genesis 22:21 (it is difficult to see why else he would be mentioned), and if Ram is the same as Aram in Genesis 22:21, then Job's friend Elihu was not only a near-contemporary of Abraham but a relative. The date of the book, however, is not as important as the content, the story of Job's suffering under God's hand and its fruits.

Is the early date of the book at all important? It is important in that it shows that the struggles of God's people in their sufferings go back to the earliest times; it shows that not only the issues but also the comforts have always been the same. It explains the lack of understanding on the part of Job and his friends of the gracious purpose of trials and suffering. It makes Job's demand for an explanation of his suffering more understandable. This Old Testament perspective is difficult for us to imagine:

> Think for a moment what it would be to encounter crushing sorrows not only without Calvary and Gethsemane and the sympathy of the incarnate Son of God, who is Himself touched with the feeling of our infirmities...with no clear views of that eternal blessedness, in comparison with which all earthly sorrow, however grievous in themselves, and long continued, are nevertheless light and momentary.[1]

---

1   Green, *The Argument of the Book of Job Unfolded*, 79–80.

Trying to put ourselves with our trials into Job's place in the Old Testament therefore should make us thankful for our New Testament blessings.

There is a great deal of misunderstanding regarding Job's struggle and his sin. There are suggestions that Job lost his faith for a time. The book, however, shows Job to be not only a believer but one with a deep understanding of God, a firm faith in God, and a confidence in God that does not waver through all his difficulties. In that, too, he is an example of believers and is commended both in Ezekiel and in James for his righteousness and for his patience.

Job's sin was not weakness of faith nor a failure to understand the equity of God's dealings with righteous and wicked. He was not troubled by the apparent prosperity of the wicked as Asaph was (Ps. 73). He did not doubt that his afflictions were from God or ever question the justice and wisdom of God in afflicting him. He did not despair of God's love and mercy. His problem, as we shall see, was different, but a problem that touches at the heart of our need for patience and peace in afflictions.

Except at the one point where he sins, he is a wonderful example to us. Even sinning he is an example of what we must not do when we suffer under the almighty hand of God and in his wonderful wisdom. Job lives on in every suffering child of God as he or she learns to submit to God's sovereign good pleasure.

Calvin sums up the lessons of the book of Job beautifully:

The story which is here written shows us how we are in the hand of God, and that it belongs to Him to order our lives and to dispose of them according to His good pleasure, and that our duty is to submit ourselves to Him in all humility and obedience, that it is quite reasonable that we be altogether His both to live and to die; and even if it shall please Him to raise His hand against us, though we may not perceive for what cause He does it, nevertheless we should glorify Him always, confessing that He is just and equitable, that we should not murmur against Him, that we should not enter into dispute, knowing that if we struggle against Him we shall be conquered.[2]

2   John Calvin, *Sermons from Job, selected and translated by Leroy Nixon* (Grand Rapids, MI: William B. Eerdmans Co., 1952), 3. Calvin preached 159 sermons on Job on weekdays from 1554 to 1555. Twenty sermons are selected in this book.

2

JOB'S CHARACTER

(Job 1:1–5)

Job 1:1–5 tells us very little about Job's outward circumstances but gives us great insight into Job's spiritual character, as does the whole story of his trials. Of his circumstances we know only that he was from the land of Uz, was fabulously wealthy, and had ten children—none of which has any bearing on what we know of his piety and faithfulness, in spite of Satan's accusations to the contrary. Scripture tells us so little of him because it focuses always on the important things.

Uz is thought to be between Damascus and the Euphrates. That would put Job in or near the area from which Abraham came and would explain his knowledge of God and his piety, for the worship of God lingered in that area at least until the end of the patriarchal era (Gen. 31:51–53). Indeed, if the dating of Job's life is accurate, then Job may very well have known Abraham's family and perhaps Abraham himself.

Job is identified as the "greatest of all the men of the east" (Job 1:3), and though that does not tell us exactly where he lived, "the east" in scripture is the whole area of Arabia and of the Fertile Crescent, which stretches from Syria to Babylon. Abraham sent his sons by Keturah, the ancestors of the Arab tribes, "unto the east country" (Gen. 25:6), and Jacob when he came to Haran "came into the land of the people of the east" (29:1). Job's three friends and Job himself were apparently from the same vast area.

He was "the greatest of all the men of the east" especially in wealth and influence (v. 3). Estimates of Job's wealth in modern money range from five to fifty million dollars, but we live in a time when wealth is estimated very differently and when animals, the foundation of Job's fortune, are much less valuable than in Job's day. However reckoned, there is no doubt that Job was wealthy beyond imagination.

Later Job speaks of his godly use of the wealth God gave him:

11. When the ear heard me, then it blessed me; and when the eye saw me, it gave witness to me:
12. Because I delivered the poor that cried, and the fatherless, and him that had none to help him.
13. The blessing of him that was ready to perish came upon me: and I caused the widow's heart to sing for joy.
14. I put on righteousness, and it clothed me: my judgment was as a robe and a diadem.
15. I was eyes to the blind, and feet was I to the lame.
16. I was a father to the poor: and the cause which I knew not I searched out. (Job 29:11–16)

It may be harder for a rich man to enter the kingdom than for a camel to go through the eye of a needle, but Job certainly showed that by God's grace it is possible. In his trials he showed, too, that he had not set his heart on his riches—that he was not a worshiper of mammon. In that he is an example to all who are blessed with material prosperity.

Of his ten children we know nothing except that they were old enough to have their own houses. The reference in Job 1:4 to the round of feasting that his children enjoyed should not be taken as a negative commentary on their spirituality. There is no indication that their behavior was anything other than their enjoying thankfully all that God had so richly given to them and their father (1 Tim. 4:4–5). Indeed, Job, in offering sacrifice for them, does not accuse them of any evildoing or impiety, but only suggests the possibility that they had sinned, as all of us do always.[1]

Those sacrifices are a further evidence of Job's piety and godliness. They compare to the prayers that Christian parents offer on behalf of their children, praying with them or for them out of a belief in the promises of God's covenant and in God's willingness to keep these promises by saving of covenantal children. Christian parents imitate Job when in praying with their children they teach them to confess their sins and seek forgiveness in the death of Christ. They imitate Job when they seek forgiveness for their children, acknowledging their immaturity as Job did: "It may be that my sons have sinned, and cursed God in their hearts." These duties are all too often neglected by parents.

Of Job's wife nothing is said until chapter 2:9–10, where she tells Job to "curse God, and die," and it is impossible to judge her character on that alone. A charitable view would be that she spoke hastily and foolishly under the immense pressure of suffering, something we

---

1   Green suggests that the word "cursed" in Job 1:5 has the idea of saying farewell to God or forgetting him in happy times (*The Argument of the Book of Job Unfolded*, 23–24).

are all inclined to do. Whatever her character, it is obvious from the sacrifices Job offered for his children that his immense wealth was not gained at the expense of his family or marital responsibilities.

Of Job's godly character God testifies in Job 1:1: "that man was perfect and upright, and one that feared God, and eschewed evil"—an amazing statement. That Job was all this by God's grace there is no doubt, but it is nevertheless what all of us should strive to be and ought to be. That he feared God is evident in the later history of Job when he humbled himself before God: "Behold, I am vile; what shall I answer thee? I will lay mine hand upon my mouth. Once have I spoken; but I will not answer: yea, twice; but I will proceed no further" (40:4–5). The fear of God shown by Job is the reverence we feel for God and the awe that overwhelms us in his presence. For us and for Job it was the spring of his uprightness and piety.[2]

It is worth noting here that the description of Job in verse 1 is God's own description of him; God calls Job perfect and upright, one who feared God and avoided evil. What a wonder, that God should thus speak of anyone, and what a motive to piety and godliness, to hear such a description of anyone.

Job's eschewing or avoiding of evil is something that is altogether lacking in our times. Too many Christians walk as close to evil as they can in the company they keep, in the music they hear, in what they watch, in their recreation and business practices, in marriage and family life, imitating the ungodly in their culture and practices. Churches, too, conduct themselves as businesses, worship is modeled on worldly entertainment, and Christians live piously for only a few hours on the Lord's day, if then. Would that there were more like Job.

---

2   Green, *The Argument of the Book of Job Unfolded*, 20–21.

That he was perfect and upright refers to his conduct. *Upright* is the opposite of groveling in sin and rolling in the gutter of evil, and *perfect* is not the same as sinless but refers to conduct that is above reproach. There are no sinless men except Jesus. By his own confession Job was a sinner: "I have sinned; what shall I do unto thee, O thou preserver of men?" (7:20); "If I justify myself, mine own mouth shall condemn me: if I say, I am perfect, it shall also prove me perverse" (9:20). *Perfect* means that Job's confession and life matched. He did not, as Calvin says, "keep a shop in the rear" to turn himself away from God.[3] Would God we were all like him in that respect. There is more to obedience than outward conformity to God's law and holiness, and Job had that, too, but it is a Christian's behavior and conduct that is seen and that either brings disgrace on God's name or magnifies it.

Ezekiel 14:14, 20 makes reference to Job's righteousness. Righteousness is the righteousness of God himself, freely imputed to unrighteous sinners through faith, the faith that unites them to Christ. Job was perfect and upright, not by his own efforts to distinguish himself before God, but alone by God's grace. His God-fearing conduct was the fruit of that imputed and gifted righteousness, the fruit of God's saving grace in Jesus Christ.

When God asks Satan, "Hast thou considered my servant Job?" the word translated *considered* could be *set thine heart on*. Satan had not done that, had not set his heart on Job, had not even really considered who and what he was by God's grace, but God had set his heart on Job in eternity, had foreknown Job in love, and that could not fail or change in the most dire circumstances. Job, like David, was a man after God's own heart, and having set his heart on Job, God would give his own Son to be Job's redeemer and

---

3 Calvin, *Sermons from Job*, 10.

would preserve Job from all Satan's wiles. It is Job's spiritual character that is emphasized in these first verses of the book therefore, not his outward circumstances, and his character is an example to us all, those untried and those severely tested. Outward circumstances do not matter, but our response to God's dealings with us, whether in prosperity or adversity, do.

What a reminder he is, too, of our need for God's correction and chastening. If he, perfect and upright, was in need of such trials, how much more we who would be afraid to set ourselves on the same spiritual level as Job. How true it is that "whom the Lord loveth he chasteneth, and scourgeth every son whom he receiveth" (Heb. 12:6).

God shows his sovereignty, too, in chastening Job. Job's uprightness did not shelter him from God's chastening hand, or mean that he was above chastening. God does as he will with his own (Matt. 20:15). His ways are not our ways or his thoughts our thoughts.

3

JOB'S FIRST TRIAL AND HIS RESPONSE

(Job 1:6–22)

The story of Job's troubles is valuable both because it illustrates God's sovereignty in trials and suffering and because it shows Satan's part in those same trials. The word *trial* in both the Old and New Testaments shows that God and Satan together are involved in our trials, though never as equals. In the Old and New Testaments the word *trial* and the word *temptation* are the same, though differently translated in English. What is a trial on God's part, that is, a testing of our faith and obedience in the fire of suffering, is on Satan's part a temptation. God tested Job, and Satan tempted him, not only in being the agent of Job's losses but as the shadowy figure behind his friends and wife whom he used to tempt Job further.

The relationship between God and Satan in trials and temptation is exquisitely revealed in Job's tale of woe in a way unmatched by other passages of scripture. The lesson is that though Satan plays a part in suffering, God is sovereign even over him and controls all things for the good of his own. The presence of both must be remembered, however: God's sovereign presence in our trials is our comfort, but Satan's presence is a reminder that we must be constant in watching and prayer so that we do not fall into temptation or sin as Job did.

The sins to which we are tempted in suffering are many. We sin by questioning God's justice and goodness, by complaining and being discontented, by thinking we deserve better than God sends us, by taking out our frustrations and discontent on others, by attempting to find a reason for our trials beyond what God reveals in his word (as Job did), by using our trials as an excuse to commit deliberate sins, by cutting ourselves off from God and from others in suffering. Satan is there to tempt us to these sins, though the lesson of Job's suffering is that we must watch diligently for his lion-like and devouring presence (1 Pet. 5:8).

God's presence in our trials is revealed in Satan's inability to do anything against Job without God's permission and in God's strictly limiting what Satan was able to do. In the first trial Satan is forbidden to put forth his hand against Job's person, though he is permitted to take everything else away from Job. That he was permitted to act against Job is not a denial of God's sovereignty. The word *permission* describes perfectly what we read in the story of Job, but there is no difference between God permitting Satan to act against Job and God himself acting, and Satan can do nothing without God's permission. Indeed, Satan is entirely in the hand of God for Job's good.

Satan comes "to offer his homage, to receive his commissions, to render his stated account of work done and service performed... in the attitude of a servant of God, and made subservient to the discipline and training of his people."[1] Satan is God's agent in the trials

---

1   Green, *The Argument of the Book of Job Unfolded*, 41, 43.

of Job and "in all his blasphemous designs he is, in spite of himself, doing the work of God. In his rebellious efforts to dethrone the Most High, he is actually paying Him submissive homage. In moving heaven and earth to accomplish the perdition of those whom Christ has ransomed, he is actually fitting them for glory."[2]

Nevertheless, we ought to tremble when we think of Satan's power, given by God to be sure, entirely controlled and directed by the Most High, but great indeed. God says to Satan, "Behold, he is in thine hand" (Job 2:6). He is the prince of this world and an enemy to be reckoned with. He was able to do Job much harm both physically and spiritually. God's sovereignty over Satan does not change that. He is an enemy to be reckoned with. Only by prayer and grace is he to be resisted and overcome.

We may not dismiss Satan's presence in our lives as of no account. He is able to do us much harm: "Be sober, be vigilant; because your adversary the devil, as a roaring lion, walketh about, seeking whom he may devour: whom resist stedfast in the faith, knowing that the same afflictions are accomplished in your brethren that are in the world" (1 Pet. 5:8–9).

Yet Satan himself is in God's hand as Job was, with God's permission in Satan's hand. This comes out especially in Job 1:12, where Satan invites God to put forth his hand and touch Job's possessions and family. When God says to Satan, "All that he hath is in thy power" (v. 12), God makes it clear that Satan is merely his instrument. Satan's own words show that he himself recognized this. He was under the sovereignty of God, the hand of God reaching out to touch all that Job had. Job himself, whether aware or not of Satan's agency, recognized the fact that it was God who afflicted him and speaks of it often.

---

2   Green, *The Argument of the Book of Job Unfolded*, 63–64.

Satan's activity, even when successful, is always under God's direction and control, and we can be sure that our sins, when we fall prey to Satan, though inexcusable, are nevertheless used by our sovereign God for our good. Certainly that was true in the case of Job. Though he fell prey to the roaring lion whom we call Satan, even his sin brought him to a better confession of God's sovereignty and to a humble confession of his sin and repentance for it.

Satan's appearance in heaven is part of the story of his attack on Job. It is difficult to understand that he had access to heaven after falling, but both Job and Revelation 12 indicate that he did. So he appears before God among the unfallen angels (called "sons of God" in Job 1:6) to charge Job with the most mercenary of motives in serving God. And though Job's name comes up in the conversation between God and Satan almost as an afterthought, there can be no doubt that Satan's presence in heaven was the beginning of his evil attack.

Satan lives up to his name in the story of Job, for Satan means *slanderer* or *accuser*. He is Job's slanderer in his charge that Job served God only for what he got out of it—only because God had made him wealthy. That charge is slander because the true service of God cannot possibly be motivated by self-interest. It is always and only the fruit of God's amazing grace.

In Revelation 12:10 Satan is called the "accuser of our brethren…which accused them before our God day and night," and he most certainly appears in that role in Job. The pride with which Satan accuses Job before God leaves one gasping, but it is evidence of the same pride that led to his fall from heaven. So he accused others also, as he did Joshua the high priest in Zechariah 3:1. So he accused all the brethren until Christ came and took away whatever right he had to appear before God with his slanderous accusations.

17

Revelation 12:7–9 tells how his slanderous accusations came to an end. With the exaltation of our Savior, there was war in heaven between Michael and his angels and Satan and his angels. What a war between angels and demons is like we can only imagine, but it must be, in light of Jude 9, a war of words. In that war Michael and his host prevailed through the power of the ascended Lord and Satan was cast out. No doubt it was the finished work of Christ that was Satan's downfall. Christ came in the flesh, was crucified, risen, and exalted, and so there is no longer any room for such accusations as Satan brought against Job: "Who shall lay any thing to the charge of God's elect? It is God that justifieth. Who is he that condemneth? It is Christ that died, yea rather, that is risen again, who is even at the right hand of God, who also maketh intercession for us" (Rom. 8:33–34).

In Job's case Satan was still able to bring charges against one of God's elect, because Christ had not yet come in the flesh. Job had no doubt, however, that Christ was his all-in-all, and he confessed a living Savior in Job 19:25–27 who would deliver him not only from the vicious attacks of the great deceiver but from all his sins, and who would give him life everlasting in the presence of God, that is, in the very place where Satan was then standing.

Was Job aware of Satan's evil intentions and his agency in what happened? There is no evidence that he was any more aware of what Satan was doing than any of us would be. As far as Satan was concerned the purpose of God's dealings with Job was to disprove his lies and to show that obedience and service are all grace, not self-interest. In Job's case God's purpose was different. Job had to learn that it is gross sin to question God's ways with us and to demand an account of them from God. That may well mean Job never knew what happened in heaven, for God did not and would not explain himself to Job or give him a reason for what happened.

That does not mean, though, that Job was altogether ignorant of Satan's devices. Job was only a few generations removed from the fall of Adam and Eve and was as knowledgeable of Satan's evil work as we are. He might have heard the story of the fall third or fourth hand—Adam to Lamech to Noah to Shem to Job. Job would have known of Satan and his evil works, though he may well have forgotten to watch for him as we do.

Satan therefore goes out from God's presence and takes everything away from Job, making sure Job receives the news of his ill fortune in the worst possible way. The story shows Satan's great power among men and in the forces of the creation, for both the coming of Job's enemies and the whirlwind that killed Job's children were his work. It is Satan's doing, too, that Job receives the news of his losses as a series of blows. Unable to do no more or less than God willed, Satan has great power indeed!

We cannot imagine being in Job's place and losing everything in one day, including all of his children. As this is written, the nation is largely under quarantine due to the coronavirus. In parts of the world people are rioting and looting, and few find themselves able to cope with the loss of some luxuries and privileges. Sitting in a warm home with plenty to eat and access to a computer such as the one on which these words are being written, we feel deprived and ill at ease. Job bore losses that few others have experienced and showed that there was indeed none like him—that he was perfect and upright, a man who feared God and eschewed evil.

His response to his trials, though amazing, proves not Job's greatness but God's. He confessed that he had nothing that was really his own when he said, "Naked came I out of my mother's womb, and naked shall I return thither," and confessed in it his own lack of merit (Job 1:21). He ascribed all to God, who gave and took away according to his own good pleasure and will, and who is always right and good in what he does. Job worshiped God, a testimony to God's greatness and grace!

Job was not a stoic. Verse 20 tells us that he tore his robe and shaved his head, both signs of unspeakable grief, for who would not grieve the loss at once of ten dear children. Yet even in his grief, Job submitted to God and acknowledged the righteousness and the goodness of God, for God who took all away had also given, though only for a time.

Such must be the confession of every child of God in his trials. Not only must he confess that all that he has and is belongs to God who has the sovereign right to do as he pleases with his own, but also that his enjoyment of what God does give, even if it be for a little while, is a privilege and reason for thanks.

If God gives me good things and then impoverishes me, I may not complain. I must confess that it was all his anyway. If God gives me health and then takes it away, I may not be discontent but must acknowledge that my very existence is a gift from him. If God gives me a child and then takes that child away, I must not be angry with him but confess that it was a privilege to have that child for a short time and be thankful for the short time that child was in my arms and my home. What Job did in his trials I must do in mine.

The last verse of the chapter tells us that Job did not sin in his response to his trials and that he did not charge God foolishly. To charge God is to accuse him of injustice and unrighteousness in his dealing with us. That can be done in words when we complain and question, but is more often done by despondency, by unhappiness and discontent. These, though they are not openly directed against God, nevertheless amount to a charge of injustice. Job's response is amazing in light of what happened to him and to his family, and a great example to us who are inclined to grumble at the slightest inconvenience.

Such a response is rooted in the grace of God in Jesus Christ. Nothing else can make me thankful in prosperity and patient in adversity but the blessed knowledge that I am not my own but have been given, in eternal love, by the shedding of blood and the sovereign work of the Spirit to someone else.

4

JOB'S SECOND TRIAL AND HIS RESPONSE

(Job 2:1–10)

Having failed in his first attempt to prove his slanderous accusations that Job served God only out of self-interest, Satan
appears once again in heaven as the accuser of the brethren, the
great slanderer and liar. He brings the same accusation, this time
focusing not on Job's possessions and family, for he had lost all, but
on Job's own life and health: "Skin for skin, yea, all that a man hath
will he give for his life" (Job 2:4).

There is a certain truth in what Satan says. Ordinarily it is
true that a man will give everything for his life. We see that when
men sacrifice family and marriages for their own quality of life
as they view it. We see it in the efforts men put forth to preserve
their life and health. If God sends cancer then they will spend
all they have and go to any extreme to find a cure. That changes
when a person is changed by God's grace. Then he confesses that
his life is not his own but belongs to his Savior by purchase. He

will do what is necessary to preserve life and health, but his confession is always, "Whether we live…, or die, we are the Lord's" (Rom. 14:8).

That Satan does not give up in his efforts to destroy Job is a reminder of what Peter says in 1 Peter 5:8: "Your adversary the devil, as a roaring lion, walketh about, seeking whom he may devour." Satan does not give up when he has reduced Job to poverty, killed his children, and destroyed Job's health, but uses Job's friends and his wife against him. Resisting him, then, is something that must be done repeatedly. Often we give in to temptation because of his persistence, finally, as it were, throwing up our hands in despair. What Satan cannot win by direct assault is often won by long siege.

In the face of Satan's accusations stands God's word concerning Job, a repetition of what God had said previously and a testimony to God's unchangeableness and faithfulness: "Hast thou considered my servant Job, that there is none like him in the earth, a perfect and an upright man, one that feareth God, and escheweth evil?" But God adds, "Still he holdeth fast his integrity, although thou movedst me against him, to destroy him without cause" (Job 1:8; 2:3). Job was and would remain a perfect and upright man, not because he was better than others, but because God does not change. He had chosen and redeemed Job, and nothing Satan tried would change that.

With God's righteous permission Satan immediately afflicts Job with what may have been a kind of leprosy, perhaps black leprosy or elephantiasis. This disease involves unbearable itching (2:7–8), worm-eaten ulcers (7:5), deterioration of bones and flesh (30:17), wasting away (13:28), blackening and falling off of skin and fever (30:30), and terrifying nightmares (7:14). His own friends, when they came, did not recognize him (2:12). Whatever disease he had, it must have been a kind of living death. In light of what Moses would later write in Deuteronomy 28:35, it may have been viewed by many—including Job's friends—as the judgment of God: "The LORD shall smite thee in the knees, and in the legs, with a sore botch that cannot be healed, from the soles of thy feet unto the top of thy head."

It is at this point that Job's wife tells him to "curse God, and die" (Job 2:9). Her words do not make an unbelieving woman of her, but only show her to be weak and sinful as we are and as Job was. Calvin reminds us here of an important truth: "God permits that men fail us…in order that we may run back so much sooner to Him."[1] We do not read of her again, but Job's words should have weight: "Thou speakest as one of the foolish women speaketh" (v. 10). His words suggest that she was not, in Job's eyes, one of the foolish women, but a godly and pious woman who spoke foolishly under the pressure of the trials that affected her as much as they affected Job, for she was now also impoverished and had lost all her children. He takes the time to instruct her, too, as every godly husband ought to do.

Job's words to her are for us also: "What? shall we receive good at the hand of God, and shall we not receive evil?" (2:10). That is the confession of one who knows himself to be a sinner, without any standing before God, who deserves nothing but eternal wrath and judgment. *Good* and *evil* are not here moral good and evil but good things and trials. In speaking of God's right to enrich and impoverish, to give good health and to send illness, to prosper and to send adversity, Job acknowledges not only God's sovereignty as the one who has the right to do as he will with his own—that "all

---

1   Calvin, *Sermons from Job*, 105.

things come, not by chance, but by his fatherly hand"[2]—but also his own unworthiness to receive any good at all from God. All he and we deserve is evil.

That Job did not "sin with his lips" (Job 2:10) does not mean that he did sin in other ways under the pressure of trials. It does not mean he sinned in his heart or thoughts, nor does it mean that he was angry and discontented with what God had done to him. Instead of complaining or charging God foolishly he confessed God's sovereign right to deal with us as he wills. Job maintained his integrity before God and is an example of submission and trust to us. He did not do what Satan had said he would do. He did not curse God and turn away from him. He did not serve God for gain.

---

2   Heidelberg Catechism A 27, in *The Confessions and the Church Order of the Protestant Reformed Churches* (Grandville, MI: Protestant Reformed Churches in America, 2005), 94.

5

THE COMING OF JOB'S THREE FRIENDS

(Job 2:11–13)

When Job's three friends heard of his troubles they came to visit him, as friends ought to do. We know next to nothing about them except their names. Genesis 36:10–11 mentions an Eliphaz, son of Esau, who had a son Teman. Perhaps this Eliphaz the Temanite was related to that Teman. Genesis 25:2 names a certain Shuah, a grandson of Abraham by Keturah. Perhaps Bildad the Shuhite was his relative. The only Naamah in the Bible was the sister of Jabal, Jubal, and Tubal-cain, but it is difficult if not impossible to connect Zophar with her. We do not know whether the fourth friend, Elihu, who suddenly appears in chapter 32, was one of their company or came on the scene later, though his ancestry also suggests the time of Abraham and some connection with the covenantal line.

What these names do confirm is that Job was a contemporary or near-contemporary of Abraham and that the knowledge and fear of God had not disappeared outside the family of Abraham. All of these men show themselves to be men who knew the true God and worshiped him, as Job's prayers for them and their own repentance prove (Job 42:8–9). Yet, under the sovereign control of God, Satan uses them to try Job a third time and to make his suffering worse.

How are we to understand their speeches to Job, which God calls folly and for which he condemns them (Job 42:8)? A careful reading of their words shows a deep knowledge of God and reverence for him. What they say is not in itself wrong. Calvin calls it "pure truth" and the "foundations of religion."[1] They do not lie as Satan did, but though their words are factually correct they are misapplied in the case of Job and therefore are folly. Misinterpreting and misapplying the word of God is sin against the third commandment, the sin of taking God's name in vain, according to the Westminster Larger Catechism question and answer 113.[2] It is as much a sin as lying. God's later condemnation of their speeches confirms this.

Job 4:8–9, 5:17–18, and 11:7–10 are good examples of the truth misapplied to Job. In chapter 4:8–9, Eliphaz talks of God's judgment on those who "plow iniquity, and sow wickedness [and] reap the same." Eliphaz says, "By the blast of God they perish, and by the breath of his nostrils are they consumed." That is true but wrong in its application. He goes on in chapter 5:17–18 to say, "Behold, happy is the man whom God correcteth...for he maketh sore, and bindeth up: he woundeth, and his hands make whole." A great truth, but in the context, misinterpreted with reference to

---

1 Calvin, *Sermons from Job*, 5.
2 "Larger Catechism: The Orthodox Presbyterian Church", accessed March 23, 2021, https://opc.org/lc.html

Job. In chapter 11, Zophar makes a marvelous confession of God's incomprehensibility and sovereignty, but falls short of the truth not in what he says but in using it to insist that Job had sinned against God.

There is a warning for us in that. It is easy to think that because we quote the word of God, our words must be true and right; but misapplying them is as great a sin as misquoting them. In the case of Job's friends, their sin was such that atoning sacrifice and intercessory prayer were necessary. We commit their sin and need forgiveness when we apply the word of God to others and not to ourselves as we ought to do. We commit their sin when we use the word of God to condemn others harshly, unjustly, and without a hearing. We commit their sin when we use God's word to number fellow believers among the ungodly and unbelieving, banishing them from our hearts and lives. The word must be handled carefully and not deceitfully.

Job's sad condition was evident to his friends Eliphaz, Bildad, and Zophar even before they were with him, and their reaction to his suffering is a commentary on what he had experienced. From afar they did not even recognize him. When they were in his presence, not only did they indulge in the usual expressions of grief, tearing their clothes and sprinkling dust on their heads, but were left speechless for seven days and nights. They felt, at first, as we often do in the presence of suffering, that mere human words are inadequate. Perhaps it was the magnitude of his suffering that made them think that Job was under God's judgment. When they first arrived their grief and pity were real. Their conviction that Job's condition was God's judgment for sin developed and hardened as they began to speak, attempting to comfort Job, pity turning gradually to frustration and anger when Job would not listen to their charges of sin.

In the end these three friends made Job's trials worse by accusing him falsely. They were, as Job himself called them, "miserable comforters" (Job 16:2). Nevertheless, God had his own purpose in bringing them to Job at such a difficult time and in using them the way he did, wrong as they were. God, through them, brought Job to the wonderful confession of Christ his redeemer in Job 19:25–27. He used them, too, to bring Job to a better understanding of his own sovereignty and glory. Through their efforts Job learned anew that God is GOD and that he is the God of his people.

This is the third stage in Job's trials, and, though unwittingly, his friends are used by Satan, the great adversary, to increase Job's troubles beyond bearing. Satan is the accuser of the brethren not only in heaven before God but through these friends of Job. They serve as his instruments by their accusations. Through them he does what he did in the garden to our first parents and what he did to our Lord in his three temptations: twisting the word of God to his own nefarious purposes. Calvin names them the servants of Satan: "When the devil thus lights the fire he also pumps the bellows, that is to say, he finds men who are his own to continually prick us and to lengthen and augment the illness."[3] These men did not belong to Satan but were used by him, to their shame and ours, for Satan often uses us as he used them.

Nevertheless, in the sovereign purpose of God, Job's three friends also learned something about God and about the word of God, though that word was still unwritten. They learned by sin and sacrifice, by prayer and forgiveness, that our redeemer lives.

---

3   Calvin, *Sermons from Job*, 4.

6

JOB'S LAMENT

(Job 3)

After the arrival of his friends, Job is the first to speak. He laments the day of his birth, wishing he were dead rather than alive: "There [in death] the wicked cease from troubling; and there the weary be at rest" (Job 3:17). The word *lament* is better than the word *curse* found in verse 1, which leaves a very wrong impression of rebellion against God and blasphemy against his name. Job is guilty of neither. His lament is an outpouring of grief that expresses his desire to see an end of his troubles.

His grief is no more than the grief of any parent who has lost a child or of anyone who suffers constant pain or who has lost everything, though it is expressed in language that sounds excessive to our delicate ears. His desire to die is no more than the desire expressed by many elderly saints who have nothing left in this life, who are weary of life and only want to go to their eternal home.

Job's grief is neither stoicism nor murmuring against God. Stoicism despises the chastening of the Lord; murmuring is not much different from fainting. We are warned against both: "My son, despise not thou the chastening of the Lord, nor faint when thou art rebuked of him" (Heb. 12:5). Job neither fainted nor rebelled, but he did not understand, not yet, what follows in verse 6: "For whom the Lord loveth he chasteneth, and scourgeth every son whom he receiveth."

Should Job have lamented the day of his birth and wished for death? Probably not, but it is not uncommon for God's people under the pressure of trials to say things that they should not say. Think of Elijah under the juniper tree or of Jeremiah and his troubles, how both had given up. In such circumstances, God does not deal with us harshly or rebuke us for every ill-spoken word, just as he never brings this matter up to Job. He rebukes Job for his great sin of calling God to account but not for lamenting the day of his birth, no more than he rebuked Elijah further than saying to him, "What doest thou here?" (1 Kings 19:13).

There is no evidence in what Job says that he had abandoned his wonderful confession, "The LORD gave, and the LORD hath taken away; blessed be the name of the LORD" (Job 1:21), no indication that he had ceased worshiping God as he had worshipped before he heard of his losses, no charging God foolishly. It is common in the face of great troubles and trials that one is at first numb to what has happened and does not really sense the enormity of it all, and only when the numbness wears off does one feel the pain and grief. That is what happens to Job.

The key verses in this chapter are verses 20–23. There Job confesses that it is God who hedged him in and who had not explained his ways to Job. He is saying, "God did this to me and I do not understand it, but it is his hand I see in all that has happened," really no different than the confession of chapter 1:21 or chapter 2:10. He also speaks of light, and in the book of Job that word never refers just to the light of day, but to the enlightenment that God gives when he opens blind eyes to the truth.

Job had that light. He was not one whose "light...shall be put out, and the spark of his fire shall not shine" (18:5). He was not one of those who "grope in the dark without light" (12:25), not one of the wicked and unbelieving, though his friends eventually charged him with such crimes. It was by the light that he could see the hand of God in his troubles, and by the same light that he confessed the righteousness of God and the sovereignty of God in God's dealing with him. In that light he knew that his redeemer lived and that he would someday see God.

That light Job never lost, but the light he had did not explain God's ways with him. He knew his friends were wrong when they charged him with gross sin and insisted that what had happened to him was punishment for sin, but he was left with that age-old question, Why? He raises that question in chapter 3:23, "Why is light given to a man whose way is hid, and whom God hath hedged in?" and would raise it again until it became his sin.

God's only answer to that question would be, "I am God." That answer would not come and humble Job until he had faced the charges of his friends and the question of whether indeed his troubles were the direct result of a specific sin and therefore also God's judgment on him. They were not, and Job would insist they were not and would confess the saving grace of his redeemer as proof.

Almost always that question has to be faced in our trials: "What have I done to deserve this?" "Is God angry with me?" "Hath God forgotten to be gracious? hath he in anger shut up his tender mercies?" (Ps. 77:9). The only answer to that question is Job's answer, "I know that my redeemer liveth" (Job 19:25). Nevertheless, faith in our redeemer is not an explanation of God's ways with us. God will not explain his ways except to tell us that his ways are not our ways (Isa. 55:9). When we ask why, God does not answer and will not answer, for that question may not even be asked, lest we put ourselves in the place of God and forget that we are but dust and ashes.

So we learn from the example of Job to be patient in adversity, putting all our confidence in our redeemer and his saving work. So we learn from God himself, who tells us the story of Job, that we must unquestioningly and humbly submit ourselves to him whose thoughts are not our thoughts and whose ways are not our ways. When we have forgotten the exhortation of Hebrews 12:5, when our knees are feeble and our hands hang down under the pressure of suffering, then God, using Job as an example, says to us, "God dealeth with you as with sons; for what son is he whom the father chasteneth not? (v. 7).

Part Two

THE FIRST ROUND
OF SPEECHES

7

THE FIRST SPEECH
OF ELIPHAZ

(Job 4–5)

The Temanites were known for their wisdom: "Concerning Edom, thus saith the LORD of hosts; Is wisdom no more in Teman? is counsel perished from the prudent? is their wisdom vanished?" (Jer. 49:7). But Eliphaz, the first of Job's friends to speak, shows a notable lack of wisdom in his answer to Job. He sets himself and the other friends not in wisdom's way but in folly's way, in a way where he and the others would sin against God.

Much of what Eliphaz says is true. What he says in Job 5:17–18 is fundamental to our humble and patient submission to God: "Behold, happy is the man whom God correcteth: therefore despise not thou the chastening of the Almighty: for he maketh sore, and bindeth up: he woundeth, and his hands make whole." True, but Eliphaz means that the chastening Job endured was for specific sins, thus twisting the blessed truth of these verses to make it an accusation.

It is true that God chastises us because we are sinners, that he chastises us to bring us to repentance, that he chastises us to correct us and hold us back from evil. That is a far cry from what Eliphaz says, that the man whom God chastises is guilty of gross unrepented sin. When Eliphaz suggests that gross sin on Job's part is the reason for his troubles, it is only a suggestion and is made very cautiously, but becomes the foundation for further and more extreme charges. Green puts it well:

> This point is so skillfully put, that what he actually says can scarcely be objected to: it is only what he implies, by offering this as the solution of the case in hand. He brings no harsh or doubtful charge against Job. He expresses no suspicion, and apparently entertains none. His plea is rather based on the assumption that Job is really what he has ever been supposed to be in uprightness and the devout fear of God.[1]

Eliphaz makes this charge, however indirectly, in chapter 4:7–8: "Remember, I pray thee, who ever perished, being innocent? or where were the righteous cut off? Even as I have seen, they that plow iniquity, and sow wickedness, reap the same." He simply states this as a general principle, and as such it is true. He makes no specific application to Job, but the implication is obvious: this is what Job must take to heart, and in it he will find the answer to his difficulties. He makes the same veiled charge in chapter 5:6–7: "Although affliction cometh not forth of the dust, neither doth trouble spring out of the ground; yet man is born unto trouble, as the sparks fly upward."

---

1 William Henry Green, *The Book of Job Unfolded*, rev. and ed. Michael J. McHugh (Arlington Heights, IL: Christian Liberty Press, 1996), 47.

It is worth noting that Eliphaz brings up, though indirectly, the death of Job's children as proof of his wickedness, saying that the foolish man's "children are far from safety, and they are crushed in the gate, neither is there any to deliver them" (5:4). Later, in chapter 8, Bildad focuses on this and cruelly finds in their death clear proof of Job's sin.

This is not only a false accusation but also a misinterpretation of God's providences, for while it is true as a general principle that sin and suffering go together, it does not mean that God in afflicting someone is punishing him for specific sins he has committed. Suffering began with Adam's and Eve's sin and is the lot of all their fallen children, the consequence of sin. We would not suffer if we were not sinners, and when our sin is finished our suffering will be finished also. God, however, has other purposes in suffering than inflicting punishment for specific sins. Jesus establishes this in John 9:2–3 in the case of the man born blind, when, in answer to the question of the disciples, "Who did sin, this man, or his parents?" Jesus says: "Neither hath this man sinned, nor his parents: but that the works of God should be made manifest in him."

There are cases where suffering is the direct result of specific sins: AIDS is usually, though not always, the consequence of homosexual activity, and cirrhosis of the liver the consequence of drunkenness. Permanent physical injury may result from carelessness and speeding on the highway, but these instances do not prove a general rule. No one may conclude that a person who has AIDS is guilty of homosexuality, not without further evidence—that person may have contracted the disease in the course of working in the hospital or as a laboratory technician. In the Old Testament the leper was not necessarily a greater sinner than others, though leprosy was a fearsome picture of sin and had enormous social consequences.

Misinterpreting God's providences is going beyond what God says in his word and drawing conclusions about oneself and others that are not warranted by what the word teaches. Some do this when they use certain happenings in their lives as the reason for a certain course of action, even when that course of action puts them in conflict with commands of scripture. Job's friends do it when they conclude from God's providential dealing with Job that he was guilty of gross sin, a conclusion that is often drawn about self or others today in spite of clearer revelation. If Job is indeed one of the earliest books of the Bible, then it is understandable that his friends so misinterpreted his circumstances, but it is inexcusable today in light of John 9 and other passages.

Does that mean that one does not feel that he has sinned when trials come? Under suffering one feels very keenly his sin and sinfulness, and if he has committed sins that remain unconfessed, he ought to repent of them under the pressure of suffering. Even then, however, there is no necessary connection between his sins and his suffering.

Does the danger of misinterpreting God's providences mean we ought not examine ourselves when trials come? We ought to do so, not only when we are suffering, but always, and we will always find sins that need to be brought to the throne of grace. But unless there is an unmistakable connection between our sins and our suffering, we are unwise to draw a connection, and others are wrong to do so also.

Is confession of sin important when we are suffering? Indeed it is, for confession of our sins will bring us to the cross and there to the conviction that our redeemer lives. That will be our only comfort in our trials, for there is no other comfort.

Having implied a certain blood guiltiness on Job's part, Eliphaz tells him to go to God with the matter: "I would seek unto God, and unto God would I commit my cause: which doeth great things and unsearchable; marvellous things without number" (Job 5:8–9).

In addition to suggesting that Job was guilty of sin and under the judgment of God, Eliphaz is guilty of uncharitableness and lack of sympathy. He tells Job that he does not expect Job to listen to him, though Job has brought words of comfort to others in their need. He sees in Job's great grief not a need for comfort but a failure to apply to himself the comfort he had given others:

2. If we assay to commune with thee, wilt thou be grieved? but who can withhold himself from speaking?
3. Behold, thou hast instructed many, and thou hast strengthened the weak hands.
4. Thy words have upholden him that was falling, and thou hast strengthened the feeble knees.
5. But now it is come upon thee, and thou faintest; it toucheth thee, and thou art troubled. (Job 4:2–5)

Thus Eliphaz begins a round of speeches that will only increase Job's grief. Eliphaz is indeed a miserable comforter! May God spare us from ever being such comforters. Yet the speech of Eliphaz and those of the other friends drive Job to God and to the cross of our Savior, where he finds his refuge and where we must find it too.

8

JOB'S RESPONSE TO ELIPHAZ

(Job 6–7)

Job's response to the charges of Eliphaz is shocked and unbelieving: "To him that is afflicted pity should be shewed from his friend; but he forsaketh the fear of the Almighty. My brethren have dealt deceitfully as a brook, and as the stream of brooks they pass away" (Job 6:14–15); "Yea, ye overwhelm the fatherless, and ye dig a pit for your friend" (v. 27). He even accuses them of being afraid to face the fact that God afflicted him for no discernible reason, lest God do the same to them: "For now ye are nothing; ye see my casting down, and are afraid" (v. 21). He expresses again the greatness of his grief and his desire to die (vv. 1–13) but cannot believe that Eliphaz is so unmoved by his suffering and so lacking in understanding that he comes with words of reproach instead of comfort.

Job's response is for the most part a denial of the charges of Eliphaz. He addresses himself first to Eliphaz, who as a friend ought to have known better, and then to God who knows all. He challenges Eliphaz to prove his charges: "Teach me, and I will hold my tongue: and cause me to understand wherein I have erred. How forcible are right words! but what doth your arguing reprove?" (vv. 24–25). He denies that there is any truth in the insinuations of Eliphaz: "Now therefore be content, look upon me; for it is evident unto you if I lie. Return, I pray you, let it not be iniquity; yea, return again, my righteousness is in it. Is there iniquity in my tongue? cannot my taste discern perverse things?" (vv. 28–30).

He follows the same line in chapter 7, first expressing his grief and trouble (vv. 1–10) but then directing his complaint to God (vv. 11–21) instead of Eliphaz. He acknowledges himself a sinner, as all must do before God (v. 20), but insists that if he is guilty of gross and unrepented sin it is also sin that God has not forgiven:

20. I have sinned; what shall I do unto thee, O thou preserver of men? why hast thou set me as a mark against thee, so that I am a burden to myself?
21. And why dost thou not pardon my transgression, and take away mine iniquity? for now shall I sleep in the dust; and thou shalt seek me in the morning, but I shall not be. (vv. 20–21)

With these words he expresses his belief that for whatever reason God has sent such suffering, it is too much to be borne: "My days are swifter than a weaver's shuttle, and are spent without hope. O remember that my life is wind: mine eye shall no more see good" (7:6–7). That is not a lack of faith but what we all experience under the hand of God, for though he promises that he will never tempt us above what we are able (1 Cor. 10:13), he often tests us to the very limits of our endurance so that what we go through seems to be beyond bearing. Nor must Job be condemned for his complaint. Even his Lord would later pray in the garden, "If it be possible, let this cup pass from me" (Matt. 26:39).

Striking in this speech of Job, which seems so utterly hopeless, is the fact that he turns to God in his grief and trouble and continues to do so until his darkness becomes light. Perhaps the writer of Psalm 18 was thinking not only of himself but also of Job when he wrote, "In my distress I called upon the Lord, and cried unto my God: he heard my voice out of his temple, and my cry came before him, even into his ears" (v. 6). That is what Job does, and in bringing his complaint to God his faith and his righteousness are evident and he begins the long road to peace. We, too, when there is no one else to whom to go, go to God. When no one else understands, God in Christ is touched with the feeling of our infirmities. When no one else will hear, God hears in mercy. When men have no answers, God in due time gives his word.

9

THE FIRST SPEECH OF BILDAD

(Job 8)

Bildad, in his first speech, is less reserved than Eliphaz. He does not openly accuse Job of sin but picks up on Eliphaz's mention of Job's children and finds in Eliphaz's suggestion that they had sinned the reason for Job's troubles: "Thy children have sinned against him, and he [has] cast them away for their transgression" (v. 4). He blames their supposed sin on Job: "If thou wert pure and upright; surely now he would awake for thee, and make the habitation of thy righteousness prosperous" (v. 6). It is hard to imagine anything more cruel, though he and the others were far from finished with Job.

What Bildad says is not only cruel, but wicked, for Bildad offers no proof of sin on Job's part or on the part of his children. Bildad is fishing for evidence of Job's unfaithfulness, not presenting evidence. No one may suspect, much less charge another with sin without proof. It is Bildad who perverts judgment, not God or Job (v. 3).

45

Convinced, then, that Job's troubles are the judgment of God, Bildad begins to speak of Job as though he were an unbeliever and a hypocrite. He does not directly call Job a hypocrite but says, "Can the rush grow up without mire? can the flag grow without water? Whilst it is yet in his greenness, and not cut down, it withereth before any other herb. So are the paths of all that forget God; and the hypocrite's hope shall perish: whose hope shall be cut off, and whose trust shall be a spider's web" (vv. 11–14). Thus he points the finger at Job.

Bildad as much as calls Job a liar in verse 2 and an evildoer in verse 20: "Behold, God will not cast away a perfect man, neither will he help the evil doers." He comes back again to Job's family and says, "He shall lean upon his house, but it shall not stand: he shall hold it fast, but it shall not endure" (v. 15), insinuating again that Job's troubles are the result of family unfaithfulness.

Bildad is the most outspoken and pitiless of Job's friends. What he says of God and men is true but is grossly misapplied in Job's case. His cruelty to Job is common, though, for today, too, many will accuse those who are suffering of a weak faith, of some secret sin, of bringing their trials upon themselves. They are modern-day Bildads.

We learn from Bildad's words the difficulty of interpreting God's providences and the danger of doing so. Only when those providences are unmistakably connected with the circumstances of our lives may we or anyone else draw a connection. Our conduct and the conduct of others must be judged in the light of God's word and not in connection with what happens to us. We must be especially careful in judging others when suffering and troubles come their way, for we know little of their lives and nothing of their hearts.

Bildad exhorts Job to seek God and pray to him (v. 5), but even that is misdirected, for Bildad means that Job should go to God in repentance for some great and secret sin. Job was already finding his refuge in God, but Bildad had something else in mind.

Calvin sums up and critiques Bildad's speech thus:

> We have previously seen that Bildad, supporting the argument that God is just, poorly applied it when he stopped with the statement that God punishes men according as they have deserved. Now (as we have already seen) this is not an equitable rule. God sometimes spares and supports the wicked; sometimes He chastises those whom He loves and treats them with much greater severity than those who are entirely incorrigible.[1]

All theologizing that equates health and prosperity with the blessing of God misses this point. So do we when under chastisement we say, "What have I done? Why is God doing this to me?" If his chastisement brings sins to mind that we have not confessed and forsaken, as it often does, then we must deal with those sins, but even then it is difficult, if not impossible, to make a connection between God's providences and the sins we have committed. As sinners we deserve far worse than what happened to Job. We may even be guilty of unrepented sin, but chastisement does not necessarily come as our just desserts for specific sins.

---

1 Calvin, *Sermons from Job*, 46–47.

10

JOB'S RESPONSE TO BILDAD

(Job 9–10)

Responding to Bildad, Job refutes Bildad's charges, but for the most part he addresses himself not to Bildad but to God. That is the striking thing about Job's responses: always and again he turns to God, and in turning to God he eventually finds his peace in God. Still troubled and distressed, he is nevertheless sure that God hears. In that, too, he is an example of believers who must learn that there is no one else to whom they can go but God himself. To turn from him in their troubles is the worst thing they can do, though that happens. Turning to him in prayer, seeking refuge in him, they will find their peace, for he is a refuge to all who are in need: "Yea, in the shadow of thy wings will I make my refuge, until these calamities be overpast" (Ps. 57:1). Even while we are still questioning, troubled, afraid, discouraged, and fainting he is our safety.

It often happens that those to whom God sends great troubles become bitter, make an idol of their grief, are angry with God, do not submit to him, and turn away from him. They do not sing or pray and find it difficult to worship God. Family and personal devotions become a burden, and they become critical of those who try to encourage and help them. Job does not do that but practices what he preached when his troubles first overwhelmed him.

In answer to Bildad, he acknowledges the impossibility of a man ever being justified before God. He acknowledges that not as proof that his sin or his children's sins were the cause of his suffering, but as a well-known truth. Bildad's charges of sin are refuted by Job's words, spoken to God, "Thou knowest that I am not wicked" (Job 10:7). God, not Bildad, is his judge, and he is confident that before the judgment seat of God he is not guilty, not only because he knows his redeemer, but because he knows Bildad is wrong. Such is the answer of a good conscience, though no doubt Job's troubles brought to mind his sins and sinfulness: "I am afraid of all my sorrows, I know that thou wilt not hold me innocent" (9:28).

Acknowledging God's sovereignty, Job insists that God sends suffering both to the righteous and to the wicked. A man may suffer because he is a sinner, but he may also suffer because he is a saint. That truth Job saw clearly: "This is one thing, therefore I said it, He destroyeth the perfect and the wicked. If the scourge slay suddenly, he will laugh at the trial of the innocent. The earth is given into the hand of the wicked: he covereth the faces of the judges thereof; if not, where, and who is he?" (9:22–24). He would not be God if he did not judge the wicked, but he would not be God either if he did not do it in his own time and in his own way. And because he is God he sometimes prospers them before judging them, not to show them mercy but to set them in slippery places (Ps. 73:18).

He acknowledges, too, God's sovereignty in the beautiful words of chapter 9:4–10, words that presage what God will say to him when all the speeches are finished (compare 38:31–35). Job acknowledges God's strength, his inscrutability, his sovereign right to do as he pleases, but he misses one crucial aspect of God's sovereignty and in missing it falls into sin. Job forgets that God is God and Job but a creature, who has no right to call God to account by demanding of God an explanation of his trials.

God never does give Job an explanation. He never tells Job what went on in heaven before Job's life was turned upside down. He never tells Job about Satan and his machinations or of his own sovereign purpose in testing Job so severely. He simply reminds Job that he is God and insists that Job must submit and humble himself on that ground alone. Job had to learn the lesson of Romans 9:20: "Nay but, O man, who art thou that repliest against God? Shall the thing formed say to him that formed it, Why hast thou made me thus?"

Job raises that matter in his response to Bildad. Still speaking to Bildad, that is Job's point when he says:

12. Behold, he taketh away, who can hinder him? who will say unto him, What doest thou?
13. If God will not withdraw his anger, the proud helpers do stoop under him.
14. How much less shall I answer him, and choose out my words to reason with him?
15. Whom, though I were righteous, yet would I not answer, but I would make supplication to my judge.
16. If I had called, and he had answered me; yet would I not believe that he had hearkened unto my voice. (Job 9:12–16)

Job understands that God does not always answer our complaints, that he must not call God to account, but that is exactly what he wants to do in demanding an explanation from God. He understands that he cannot speak to God as an equal, that he cannot call in a mediator (daysman) to judge between himself and God: "For he is not a man, as I am, that I should answer him, and we should come together in judgment. Neither is there any daysman betwixt us, that might lay his hand upon us both" (9:32–33). Job insists to Bildad that he only wants to "make supplication" to God (v. 15), but he transgresses his own words in seeking an answer from God.

Turning, then, to God in chapter 10, Job brings up the matter of his sinfulness and admits his sin, but he also insists that he has not committed any great sin against God. Believing that he is not guilty of gross, unrepented sin, the heart of his complaint is: "Shew me wherefore thou contendest with me" (v. 2). Job was right in refuting the charges of Eliphaz and Bildad, but in rejecting their charges of sin, he falls into sin when he demands an accounting from God. God is under no obligation to explain his ways to men, and no man has the right to demand an explanation. To do so is to put oneself in the judgment seat and God at the bar. It is to set oneself in the place of God and to drag God down from his place. It is not only presumption of the worst kind but also sin. The word *why*, addressed to God, ought never to be uttered.

Job continues to raise this issue until God comes to him and shows him his fault. Only then does he realize what he had done and repent of his evil. At this point he is still puzzled that God did not and would not answer: "Lo, he goeth by me, and I see him not: he passeth on also, but I perceive him not" (9:11). Job does not mean that God was not at all to be found, seen, perceived. It is evident that Job had found God and would never lose him. Job means that God is not to be found when this question is raised. God is far away when anyone questions his ways and he will not respond.

Submission to him, whether to his commands or his ways, must be unquestioning.

Questioning God's ways seems such a small thing, but it is not small in God's eyes, for he will not give his glory to another. Job had to learn that God is God. Our children learn this lesson when we refuse to answer their persistent "Why?" insisting that they must submit to our authority because we are their parents. We must all learn that lesson in relation to God. Submission is unquestioning and bows without knowing.

Yet Job brings up the heart of the matter, too, when he asks, "How should man be just with God?" (9:2). He acknowledges the great truth that we can never have any standing with God on the basis of our own works or merit. Job knew the answer to his question as we learn in chapter 19, that we are justified with God only through the work of our redeemer and only by faith in him. Yet Job misses his own point in not applying that truth to himself as Romans 5:1–5 does:

1. Therefore being justified by faith, we have peace with God through our Lord Jesus Christ:
2. By whom also we have access by faith into this grace wherein we stand, and rejoice in hope of the glory of God.
3. And not only so, but we glory in tribulations also: knowing that tribulation worketh patience;
4. And patience, experience; and experience, hope:
5. And hope maketh not ashamed; because the love of God is shed abroad in our hearts by the Holy Ghost which is given unto us.

In that confession we, with Job, rest without ever knowing the divine reason for our trials.

11

THE FIRST SPEECH
OF ZOPHAR

(Job 11)

Zophar is the last to speak, perhaps because he was the young-est of the three friends. He carries the attack on Job a step further, actually accusing Job of sin: "If iniquity be in thine hand, put it far away, and let not wickedness dwell in thy tabernacles" (Job 11:14). He encourages Job to repent of whatever wickedness he had committed and promises a return of Job's blessedness:

15. For then shalt thou lift up thy face without spot; yea, thou shalt be steadfast, and shalt not fear:
16. Because thou shalt forget thy misery, and remember it as waters that pass away:
17. And thine age shall be clearer than the noonday; thou shalt shine forth, thou shalt be as the morning.
18. And thou shalt be secure, because there is hope; yea, thou shalt dig about thee, and thou shalt take thy rest

in safety.

19. Also thou shalt lie down, and none shall make thee afraid; yea, many shall make suit unto thee. (vv. 15–19)

Zophar does not yet accuse Job of any specific sin that might be the cause of his troubles—that will come. He very plainly accuses Job of stubbornness and lying, however, in his attempts to defend himself and in his insistence that he was not guilty of any great unrepented evil: "Should thy lies make men hold their peace? and when thou mockest, shall no man make thee ashamed?" (11:3). Unbelievable effrontery! Zophar had no proof that Job had sinned and no evidence, therefore, that he was lying.

It is always wrong to accuse anyone of evildoing without proof, whether it be the evil of lying or of some other sin. God does not do that and neither may we. Such charges would be thrown out of a worldly court, and in this informal court that Job's friends have called into session, such charges should never have been voiced.

Yet Zophar says some wonderful things about God: "Canst thou by searching find out God? canst thou find out the Almighty unto perfection? It is as high as heaven; what canst thou do? deeper than hell; what canst thou know? The measure thereof is longer than the earth, and broader than the sea" (11:7–9). Such a wonderful statement of God's incomprehensibility is found in few other places in scripture. It rivals Romans 11:33–36. Zophar shows himself by such words to be a pious and godly man. He means, however, in saying this to Job, that Job was not humbling himself before such a great God by confessing his sin, whatever it was. Zophar, like the others, speaks the truth about God but misapplies it to Job.

And lest we think that Zophar's sin is small, it required sacrifice to atone for it. It was for these false charges and slander of Job that Zophar and the others were commanded by God to offer sacrifice and to go to Job and ask him to pray for them (Job 42:8).

12

JOB'S RESPONSE TO ZOPHAR

(Job 12–14)

Job's response to Zophar is sharper than his previous responses. With some sarcasm he tells Zophar and the others that they consider themselves the fountain of all wisdom. Job knows, he says, the things they have said and their attempts to teach him only add insult to injury. Turning Zophar's accusations around, he accuses Zophar and the others of pride and lying—of pride in their attempts to stand in God's place and of lying in their accusations. "Forgers of lies and physicians of no value" he calls them (Job 13:4). Job is right. Their accusations were trumped-up lies and their condemnation of Job insufferable pride:

7. Will ye speak wickedly for God? and talk deceitfully for him?
8. Will ye accept his person? will ye contend for God?
9. Is it good that he should search you out? or as one man

mocketh another, do ye so mock him?

10. He will surely reprove you, if ye do secretly accept persons.

11. Shall not his excellency make you afraid? and his dread fall upon you? (13:7–11)

Job reminds Zophar that though the wicked do not know God, the knowledge of God is easily learned by his people. Job says:

3. But I have understanding as well as you; I am not inferior to you: yea, who knoweth not such things as these?

4. I am as one mocked of his neighbour, who calleth upon God, and he answereth him: the just upright man is laughed to scorn.

5. He that is ready to slip with his feet is as a lamp despised in the thought of him that is at ease.

6. The tabernacles of robbers prosper, and they that provoke God are secure; into whose hand God bringeth abundantly. (12:3–6)

The things of God God's people can easily learn even from the creation: "But ask now the beasts, and they shall teach thee; and the fowls of the air, and they shall tell thee: or speak to the earth, and it shall teach thee: and the fishes of the sea shall declare unto thee. Who knoweth not in all these that the hand of the LORD hath wrought this?" (12:7–9). Job's friends were treating him as a spiritual inferior and mocking him by suggesting that he did not know the truth of what they had said to him. In reply Job makes a wonderful confession of the greatness and glory of God (vv. 13–25).

13. With him is wisdom and strength, he hath counsel and understanding.

14. Behold, he breaketh down, and it cannot be built again:

he shutteth up a man, and there can be no opening.

15. Behold, he withholdeth the waters, and they dry up: also he sendeth them out, and they overturn the earth.

16. With him is strength and wisdom: the deceived and the deceiver are his.

17. He leadeth counsellors away spoiled, and maketh the judges fools.

18. He looseth the bond of kings, and girdeth their loins with a girdle.

19. He leadeth princes away spoiled, and overthroweth the mighty.

20. He removeth away the speech of the trusty, and taketh away the understanding of the aged.

21. He poureth contempt upon princes, and weakeneth the strength of the mighty.

22. He discovereth deep things out of darkness, and bringeth out to light the shadow of death.

23. He increaseth the nations, and destroyeth them: he enlargeth the nations, and straiteneth them again.

24. He taketh away the heart of the chief of the people of the earth, and causeth them to wander in a wilderness where there is no way.

25. They grope in the dark without light, and he maketh them to stagger like a drunken man.

It is interesting, though, that for all his feeling insulted and mocked, Job himself still had something to learn about the greatness and glory of God. He did not know it as well as he thought, nor do any of us. Speaking of it is one thing, but showing that we truly understand God's glory and sovereignty by wholehearted submission to him is another thing. That other thing Job had to learn, and we have often to relearn.

Nevertheless, in defending himself, Job comes another step on the way to peace. The heart of his defense in answer to Zophar is his confidence in God as the God of his salvation: "Though he slay me, yet will I trust in him: but I will maintain mine own ways before him. He also shall be my salvation: for an hypocrite shall not come before him" (13:15–16). His confession is not perfect. Instead of saying, "I will maintain mine own ways before him," Job ought to have said, "For though I do not understand his ways, he is God, and his ways are always right," but his trust in God is not misplaced.

Elihu, when he finally speaks, is right in being angry with Job "because he justified himself rather than God" (32:2). That was Job's sin, and it followed from his sin of thinking that God owed him an explanation. Nevertheless, Job's words are an expression of trust in God and show clearly that Job had not lost his faith nor turned away from God, as some charge.

Job had no doubt that he was a sinner, though the charges of his friends were false. In his troubles, his iniquities prevailed against him (Ps. 65:3), as they so often do in suffering. Old sins are remembered; recent sins disturb our conscience; our sinfulness troubles us because there is a connection between sin and suffering, though not the kind of connection Job's friends wished to establish. All our troubles and sorrows are the result of sin's coming into the world and are our lot as sinners. Nevertheless, Job's confidence and ours is, "He also shall be my salvation" (Job 13:16). As Psalm 65:3 has it, "As for our transgressions, thou shalt purge them away."

Job speaks of being torn in pieces like a lion's prey and of going about carrying his own torn flesh between his teeth (Job 13:14). Nevertheless, knowing he is a sinner who deserves nothing from God, Job trusts him: "Though he slay me, yet will I trust in him" (v.

15). The believer, even at his worst state, has nowhere to go but to God. Yet Job is troubled because God refuses to answer his pleas to show the reason for his suffering. It seems to Job that God is hiding his face from Job and dealing with him as an enemy (v. 24). Job thought that an answer from God would give him peace—peace, too, as his sins came to mind.

Job was wrong. Peace for the troubled heart does not rest in understanding God's ways or being able to explain them. Peace lies in what Job had confessed but not applied to himself, the wonderful truths that God is God, and for Jesus' sake our God and Savior.

Part Three

THE SECOND
ROUND
OF SPEECHES

13

THE SECOND SPEECH
OF ELIPHAZ

(Job 15)

In his second speech Eliphaz's attitude has changed dramatically. He picks up where Zophar left off and finds in Job's attempts to defend himself clear evidence that Job is an evildoer. He not only agrees with Zophar that Job is an evildoer but starts to dig for evidence in Job's own words, wildly accusing Job of lacking the fear of God and not praying, saying, "Yea, thou castest off fear, and restrainest prayer before God" (Job 15:4).

Eliphaz finds somehow in Job's defense of himself a denial on Job's part of any sin or evil at all. Job had said, "I am not guilty of any gross and unrepented sin that is the reason for what has happened to me. These calamities are not God's judgment on me for forsaking his ways and turning to the way of wickedness." Eliphaz says, "Aha! You deny that you are a sinner! That is evidence of your wickedness, the wickedness for which God is judging you." The heart of Eliphaz's speech, then, is chapter 15:12–16, when he says:

12. Why doth thine heart carry thee away? and what do thy eyes wink at,

13. That thou turnest thy spirit against God, and lettest such words go out of thy mouth?

14. What is man, that he should be clean? and he which is born of a woman, that he should be righteous?

15. Behold, he putteth no trust in his saints; yea, the heavens are not clean in his sight.

16. How much more abominable and filthy is man, which drinketh iniquity like water?

Eliphaz is using the doctrine of man's depravity to prove specific evildoing on Job's part and in doing so implies that Job is an ungodly man. What Eliphaz says about man's depravity is not only true, but put so well that it has been quoted as a proof text for depravity (see *Westminster Confession of Faith*, chapter 6, article 3). Nevertheless, our depravity is not and cannot be the proof that we have committed a specific sin. Our depravity means that we are prone to all evil and are capable of all evil, but it is never proof that we have committed every possible sin and any specific sin. But Eliphaz says, "You are depraved, capable of all evil, and therefore you must have committed the sins with which we charge you."

Even today in the minds of some, the doctrine of total depravity means that every man must be guilty of every possible sin, and knowing that is not true, they deny man's total depravity. Man, fallen and totally depraved, is inclined to all evil, but no one has the time, the resources, the opportunity, the means to commit every sin. It is especially wicked of Eliphaz, however, to use the doctrine of man's depravity to prove Job's evildoing. Knowing Job, he ought to have known better and to have listened to his own words, "With us are both the grayheaded and very aged men, much elder than thy father" (Job 15:10).

Job's attempts to defend himself were not a denial of man's depravity and original sin. Indeed, Eliphaz's words in Job 15:14 are an echo of Job's own words in 14:4: "Who can bring a clean thing out of an unclean? not one." Job has repeatedly confessed his sinfulness and would under pressure of these charges confess also his need of a redeemer.

Eliphaz is wrong, too, in not taking Job at his word. Just as we are required to take God at his word, so we must take others at their word unless we have clear and unmistakable evidence to the contrary. The Canons of Dordt speak of those who make a profession of faith, even though their profession may not be up to our own high standards: "With respect to those who make an external profession of faith and live regular lives, we are bound, after the example of the apostle, to judge and speak of them in the most favorable manner. For the secret recesses of the heart are unknown to us."[1] Eliphaz did not do that. The other side of this obligation is that we do not think, suspect, or charge others with evildoing unless we have proof, and even then, of course, pointing out their sin must be done humbly and carefully and within the guidelines of Matthew 18. Not only must we have proof, but the proof must be sustainable. The word of God is, "In the mouth of two or three witnesses shall every word be established" (2 Cor. 13:1), and "One witness shall not rise up against a man for any iniquity, or for any sin, in any sin that he sinneth: at the mouth of two witnesses, or at the mouth of three witnesses, shall the matter be established" (Deut. 19:15). Eliphaz therefore sins against charity in his judgment of Job, in his twisting of Job's own words, and in his refusal to take Job at his word.

He concludes his speech with a long discourse, true in itself,

---

1   Canons of Dordt 3–4.15, in *Confessions and Church Order*, 169.

but misapplied to Job, on the principle that the wicked bring their own judgment on themselves. He accuses Job of blindly turning against God, like a man who is so fat he cannot see out of his own eyes and who thinks his fat will protect him from God: "For he stretcheth out his hand against God, and strengtheneth himself against the Almighty. He runneth upon him, even on his neck, upon the thick bosses of his bucklers: because he covereth his face with his fatness, and maketh collops of fat on his flanks" (Job 15:25–27).

As difficult as it is to read of how Job was treated by his friends, it is something that happens often. In controversy and disagreement, charity, kindness, and mercy are quickly forgotten. James warns us: "But if ye have bitter envying and strife in your hearts, glory not, and lie not against the truth. This wisdom descendeth not from above, but is earthly, sensual, devilish. For where envying and strife is, there is confusion and every evil work" (James 3:14–16). We need the wisdom that is from above that we may be "first pure, then peaceable, gentle, and easy to be intreated, full of mercy and good fruits, without partiality, and without hypocrisy." Then "the fruit of righteousness is sown in peace" (v. 18).

14

JOB'S RESPONSE TO ELIPHAZ

(Job 16–17)

In his response to the second speech of Eliphaz, Job has hardly anything to say to Eliphaz or to the other two friends. Indeed, one hesitates to call them friends, for they had become Job's persecutors. A sad thing it is when those who are our fellow believers do not hesitate to persecute us in deeds or words. In his response only chapter 16:1–6 and chapter 17:10 are addressed to his friends, though he makes reference to them in chapter 16:10, 20 and chapter 17:2–4. Most of what he says, even about them, is addressed to God.

Job calls them miserable comforters and their words vain. He insists that were he in their place, he would be concerned to comfort them and not make their situation worse. For the most part, though, he is done with them, and their words from this point on are largely ignored. It is shameful that they were so inept in their attempts to comfort him, but it is not unusual, and Job does the best thing by ignoring them and turning once again to God.

As far as the charges of his so-called friends are concerned, Job is confident that his troubles are "not for any injustice in mine hands: also my prayer is pure" (Job 16:17). He is convinced, as every child of God should be, that before the bar of God's justice he is not only righteous, but as a righteous man has not sinned against his righteousness. He can still pray to God and pray in the confidence that he will be heard, the practical proof of his justification.

To God, Job complains that God acts toward him as an enemy:

11. God hath delivered me to the ungodly, and turned me over into the hands of the wicked.
12. I was at ease, but he hath broken me asunder: he hath also taken me by my neck, and shaken me to pieces, and set me up for his mark.
13. His archers compass me round about, he cleaveth my reins asunder, and doth not spare; he poureth out my gall upon the ground.
14. He breaketh me with breach upon breach, he runneth upon me like a giant. (vv. 11–14)

His perception of God as an enemy is colored by God's silent refusal to explain to Job the reason for his troubles.

Job insists that God's refusal to answer his questions leaves him perishing without hope:

13. If I wait, the grave is mine house: I have made my bed in the darkness.
14. I have said to corruption, Thou art my father: to the worm, Thou art my mother, and my sister.
15. And where is now my hope? as for my hope, who shall see it?
16. They shall go down to the bars of the pit, when our rest together is in the dust. (17:13–16)

His language is excessive, but that is not the sin for which God will rebuke him.

Indeed, Job is learning that his hope and peace are not in having his questions answered but in the bare fact that God is God and that God is his redeemer. He is but one step away from the wonderful confession he makes in chapter 19 in answer to Bildad, close because he continues to turn to God in his troubles. He is learning the lesson of Psalm 73:26, the words of another troubled child of God: "God is the strength of my heart, and my portion for ever."

What a lesson for our own troubled hearts! We all must learn in our trials that God himself and nothing but God in his grace and mercy are our peace. Questioning, inquiring, searching leave the focus where it ought not be, on ourselves. Going to God is the source of peace and assurance: "In God is my salvation and my glory: the rock of my strength, and my refuge, is in God" (Ps. 62:7). Charging God foolishly and questioning his ways is not the way to peace but puts God at the bar, and he will not be put there. Humbly acknowledging that he is God and our God is the only quiet we will ever find. We must find our refuge in the rock that is too high for us (Ps. 61:2).

What a lesson, too, on the power of prayer and the value of prayer! The power of prayer is not that we can in prayer twist God's arm. For all his asking, God never answered Job's questions, but in the simple fact of drawing nigh to God in prayer, Job begins to find in God's presence the peace he so desperately needed. It is good to draw near to God (Ps. 73:28). To draw near to God in prayer is to know once again his strength, his faithfulness, and his glory and to find in him everything we need.

It is interesting that Job mentions the purity of his prayer here (Job 16:17). He does not mean, of course, that his prayers were perfect and sinless, but that his prayer, sanctified in Christ, was acceptable to God and that he was not without the assurance that his prayers were heard, even though his questions remained unanswered.

Job has no doubts that his troubles are God's hand and that God is righteous, but his complaint is still that God will not speak to him as an equal: "O that one might plead for a man with God, as a man pleadeth for his neighbour!" (16:21). Still he does not realize that by putting God to the questions he wishes to ask, he is sinning against God. Whether he sins in expressing his hopelessness and desire to die, God only knows, for God never charges him with sin in that respect. In demanding an answer to his "why" he does sin and sins grievously, and that, too, is a lesson for all of us who suffer. God will overlook the language we use in expressing our grief and sorrow, but he will not overlook our asking him to explain his ways to us.

We ought to follow the advice of Calvin and not the example of Job at this point:

> Let us pray to God that it may please Him to support us, and to spare us, knowing that we are not capable of sustaining such a burden, unless He gives us shoulders to do it. Besides, we pray to Him that He may not use such strictness against us, that we may not experience Him as a lion; but rather that He may always show that He is our Father, and that He may not punish us as we have deserved; but that He may always cause us to experience His mercy by means of our Lord Jesus Christ, in order that after we shall have been led by His Holy Spirit in this present life, He may raise us into the eternal glory of His Angels, which He has bought for us at such a price.[1]

---

1   Calvin, *Sermons from Job*, 103–4.

15

THE SECOND SPEECH OF BILDAD

(Job 18)

Having followed the suggestion of Eliphaz in his first speech that Job was guilty of some great sin, and having heard Eliphaz agree with them in carrying the matter further, Bildad and then Zophar warn Job of the judgment of the ungodly. Bildad's second speech is such a warning. He now considers Job to be one of the wicked whose light will be put out and who will be "driven from light into darkness, and chased out of the world" (18:5, 18).

Warnings are needed and must be given by parents to their children, by believers to one another, by believers to those who are yet unbelieving and ungodly, but such warnings must be given carefully. A child or a believer who has fallen into sin must be told that, apart from God's saving grace and without repentance, the way of sin is the way to hell; however, knowing neither the eternal good pleasure of God nor the heart of man, we may not number a child or a fellow believer among the ungodly or an unbeliever among the reprobate and simply consign him or her to hell.

The judgment of sinners belongs to God, and we may never put ourselves in God's place in speaking to others of their sins, real or perceived. To write off a son or daughter who is living sinfully as reprobate is to take God's place as judge. To say to a fellow believer who has sinned, "You are going to hell," is an attempt to climb onto a throne that is much too large for us. We must be very careful calling fellow believers heretics, drunkards, rebels, fornicators, idolaters, for these are the names of the ungodly. To use such names indiscriminately and by way of banishing others from our presence and God's is attempting to take God's place.

Bildad speaks of the wicked in general terms, but it is evident from the tenor of his words that he considers Job among the wicked, that is, among those who live unrepentantly and carelessly in sin. His judgment of Job is especially serious in that, as a friend of Job, he had clear evidence to the contrary and at very most should have judged Job as an erring brother.

Even those who are not saved may not be judged arrogantly and presumptuously by us. As the Canons of Dordt say, "And as to others, who have not yet been called, it is our duty to pray for them to God, who calls the things that are not as if they were. But we are in no wise to conduct ourselves towards them with haughtiness, as if we had made ourselves to differ" (cf. Job 3–4; 15).[1] It is not only presuming against God to make such judgments, but also a denial of God's sovereignty, for to whom he wills he shows mercy and whom he wills he hardens (Rom. 9:18).

Such judgments are all too common, not only in respect to

---

1   Canons of Dordt 3–4.15, in *Confessions and Church Order*, 169.

those who are sinning but even against those who disagree with us in doctrine and practice. When we consign them in words or in our hearts to the judgments of the ungodly, we stand in the place of Job's friends and commit grievous sin, sin that requires atoning sacrifice.

16

JOB'S RESPONSE TO BILDAD

(Job 19)

In his response to Bildad, Job begins to see his way through his trouble. The black clouds of fear and discouragement will not have vanished entirely when he is finished answering Bildad, but the healing sun of God's grace in Christ will have broken through those clouds. Though his questions remain unanswered and though he does not yet realize that his questions are sinful, he finds peace in the knowledge of God's redeeming grace and in the hope of the resurrection of the body. Having found peace, he continues in his remaining speeches to speak more of God than of himself and his difficulties, and so his healing continues.

Once again Job chides his friends for their lack of love and their failure to comfort him. He mentions the ten times they reproached him, though they have spoken only five times in total. Either he exaggerates and means enough is enough, or he refers to ten different charges they've made in their five speeches. In any case, he hardly bothers with them and pours out once again his complaint to God.

Two things only Job says to his friends. He tells them that even if he has sinned as they've charged, he is not going to talk about his sin to them: "And be it indeed that I have erred, mine error remaineth with myself" (Job 19:4). Their lack of charity has made that impossible. Nor will he look to any other judgment but God's, for "God hath overthrown me, and hath compassed me with his net" (v. 6). Refusing to speak any more of the charges they've leveled at him, he pleads once more for their pity (v. 21).

Not expecting their pity, and having made clear to them that his business is with God and not with them, Job again pours out his heart to God. He complains that God appears to be his enemy, evidence of which he sees in his wife, friends, relatives, servants, acquaintances, even young children, turning away from him. Job refers to them as "his [God's] troops" (v. 12), an army arrayed against him. There is no reason to believe that Job is exaggerating, and it is not uncommon that people, even Christians, avoid those who are suffering. So Job complains of loneliness but sees in his loneliness God's enmity.

Sometimes others turn away from those who are suffering because they are embarrassed by their inability to say something helpful and comforting. Sometimes they just do not want to bother. But sometimes, consciously or unconsciously, they avoid the sufferer because it seems to them, as it did to Job's friends, that the sufferer is under God's judgment. If that is the case, they make the same judgment by their actions that Job's friends did with their mouths. Whatever our motives may be, to walk by on the other side is the opposite of being a neighbor to those who are in need.

Following his complaint of loneliness, Job unexpectedly sees the light of God's grace and glory and gives a most beautiful testimony, confessing his redeemer and the hope of the resurrection of the body. His testimony does not fall short of anything in the New Testament. Job, by faith, catches a glimpse of things to come and, seeing them, forgets for a moment his troubles.

Job sees Christ as his redeemer, and though he could not possibly have understood as we do all the details and wonder of Christ's redeeming work, he nevertheless finds in Christ his hope and peace. The word he uses to describe Christ as his redeemer refers in the Old Testament to the next of kin and to his responsibility to avenge the blood of his kinfolk. Job makes confession, then, that Christ is the next of kin to his people and the avenger of their blood, by the shedding of his own blood on the cross.

Job confesses, too, that Christ is the one who lives forever: "I know that my redeemer liveth" (19:25). Living forever, Christ is also one whom Job knows personally, someone in whom he has long trusted.

Job's words do not describe Christ as the one who would be raised from the dead, the firstfruits of them that sleep (1 Cor. 15:20). Nevertheless, the resurrection of Christ is implied in Job's words of hope concerning his own resurrection. He knew what Paul would later say in 1 Corinthians 15:17–18: "And if Christ be not raised, your faith is vain; ye are yet in your sins. Then they also which are fallen asleep in Christ are perished." There is no hope of the resurrection of the body except in the resurrection of Christ, and Job's words "I know that my redeemer liveth" are a confession not only of Christ as the ever-living Son of God, but of Christ as the one who is alive from the dead. He foretells the resurrection of Christ as well as his own bodily resurrection, and those who deny that Old Testament believers had any knowledge of or hope of the resurrection are shamed by the words of Job.

Confessing Christ's resurrection from the dead, Job also looks forward to his own resurrection with words that ring in the soul of every troubled saint: "And though after my skin worms destroy this body, yet in my flesh shall I see God: whom I shall see for myself, and mine eyes shall behold, and not another; though my reins be consumed within me" (Job 19:26–27). There was no doubt in his mind that in his own body, raised and glorified, he would be in heaven with God, and that the corruption of the body after death was no obstacle to what God had promised.

He saw that this would take place at "the latter day" (19:25), the great day of judgment and of this world's end, and saw that the instrument both of judgment and of resurrection would be his redeemer. That redeemer would stand in that day upon the earth, having come from God with eternal blessing and renewal for all who believe in him.

The most remarkable thing about Job's confession is the word *liveth* (v. 25). He confesses Christ not as his coming redeemer, not as the one promised, but as one who is forever alive, the only begotten Son of God. Job's confession is similar to Jesus' own words in Revelation 1:18: "I am he that liveth, and was dead; and, behold, I am alive for evermore." Not, "I was dead and am alive," but "I am he that liveth, and was dead." Job knew that his redeemer was the ever-living God.

How did Job know these things? If, as we believe, Job lived at the time of Abraham, then he had none of the great Old Testament passages to teach him these things, for none of the scriptures had then been written. He could not open his Bible and read Psalm 16:8–11, Psalm 17:15, or Isaiah 26:19. Nevertheless he knew, as we do, by the word of God. Though there was as yet no written word of God, God had revealed these things to his people, and they were passed on from father to son. Abraham showed he knew these things when he offered Isaac and received him back from the dead in a figure. Abraham showed he knew when he buried Sarah in the land that for him was a picture of the land God had promised. Abraham saw Christ's day "and was glad" (John 8:56). Jacob knew Christ and the hope of the resurrection in Christ and showed it when he asked to be buried with Abraham, Sarah, Isaac, Rebekah, and Leah. These Old Testament believers knew of Enoch, who was "translated that he should not see death" (Heb. 11:5), and of Abel, whose sacrifice was accepted of God and who could never be forgotten by God. They knew that God is not the God of the dead but of the living, the God of Adam and Enoch and Noah and of all who believe (Luke 20:38). With Abraham they knew him who "quickeneth the dead, and calleth those things which be not as though they were" (Rom. 4:17). Job knew, too. He is one of those who died in faith, not having received the promises but having seen them afar off, and was persuaded of them and embraced them.

Job knew these things by faith, for "faith is the substance of things hoped for, the evidence of things not seen" (Heb. 11:1). Faith is sure of what the eye cannot see and of what the ear has not heard; faith is sure because it is the gift of God and because it unites us to him who is Job's and our redeemer, the one whom death cannot overcome.

Job wanted his words of protest against the charges of his friends written down and graven in the rock: "Oh that my words were now written! oh that they were printed in a book! that they were graven with an iron pen and lead in the rock for ever!" (Job 19:23–24). His hope of the resurrection, however, needs no monument, for Christ his redeemer is all he needs. His questions still unanswered, he finds hope and peace and assurance in Christ. As Green puts it, "the flukes of his anchor have taken hold of the immovable Rock of Ages."[1]

---

1   Green, *The Argument of the Book of Job Unfolded*, 182.

17

THE SECOND SPEECH OF ZOPHAR

(Job 20)

Zophar's second speech is also his last, for the accusations of Zophar and his companions will all come to nothing in the face of Job's confidence. Job reduces them to silence before Zophar has opportunity to speak again. Nevertheless, Zophar does not hesitate to accuse Job of specific evildoing, of misusing the wealth God had given him. From Eliphaz's first suggestion that Job's trouble was God's judgment for sin, to his insistence that Job's attempts to defend himself were proof that he had indeed sinned, to Bildad's counting Job among the ungodly, we come in Zophar's second speech to specific charges of sin against Job.

The charges are without ground, and such suspicions should never have entered Zophar's head. Job himself will refute them in his answer to Zophar, but these were friends who knew Job and knew his reputation, and that makes their slanders even worse. Psalter 24 asks:

Who, O Lord, with Thee abiding,
In Thy house shall be Thy guest?
Who, his feet to Zion turning,
In Thy holy hill shall rest?

The answer of the Psalter number is to the point:
He that ever walks uprightly,
Does the right without a fear,
When he speaks, he speaks not lightly,
But with truth and love sincere.
He that slanders not his brother,
Does no evil to a friend;
To reproaches of another,
He refuses to attend.[1]

Such sins of the tongue, though common, are great sins. Job's friends are doing what Satan did in God's presence and, in fact, doing Satan's work. They continue, though unwittingly, the efforts of the great slanderer to destroy Job and are heedless of his pleas for mercy. The words of James are right: "And the tongue is a fire, a world of iniquity: so is the tongue among our members, that it defileth the whole body, and setteth on fire the course of nature; and it is set on fire of hell" (James 3:6).

Though most of Zophar's speech is a warning against wickedness, echoing the words of Bildad, the main point of Zophar's charge is in Job 20:18–20:

---

1   No. 24:1–2, *The Psalter with Doctrinal Standards, Liturgy, Church Order, and added Chorale Section*, reprinted and revised edition of the 1912 United Presbyterian *Psalter* (Grand Rapids, MI: Wm. B. Eerdmans Publishing Co., 1927; rev. ed. 1995).

18. That which he laboured for shall he restore, and shall not swallow it down: according to his substance shall the restitution be, and he shall not rejoice therein.

19. Because he hath oppressed and hath forsaken the poor; because he hath violently taken away an house which he builded not;

20. Surely he shall not feel quietness in his belly, he shall not save of that which he desired.

He accuses Job of oppressing and robbing the poor and suggests that all of Job's former possessions would not be sufficient to make restitution.

In his zeal to condemn Job and find proof of evildoing, Zophar exceeds the bounds not only of love and mercy but even of common decency. Satan did not make such patently false charges against Job. In making such charges, Zophar, too, following the example of Eliphaz and Bildad, counts Job among the ungodly:

4. Knowest thou not this of old, since man was placed upon earth,

5. That the triumphing of the wicked is short, and the joy of the hypocrite but for a moment?

6. Though his excellency mount up to the heavens, and his head reach unto the clouds;

7. Yet he shall perish for ever like his own dung: they which have seen him shall say, Where is he? (Job 20:4–7)

This is shameful behavior for a child of God and yet is all too common. Everyone who loves God and the brother must pray fervently and often: "Set a watch, O LORD, before my mouth; keep the door of my lips" (Ps. 141:3).

18

JOB'S RESPONSE TO ZOPHAR

(Job 21)

Job's second answer to Zophar has a different tone than his previous speeches. There is an element of hopelessness in his previous speeches that has disappeared. The questions he directed to God have not been answered, but he has risen above the false and foolish charges of his friends and dismisses their charges, especially their references to the judgment of the ungodly, with a speech that amounts to: "I know all that; indeed, I know it better than you do."

In his response to Zophar Job eloquently describes the end of those who perish under the judgment of God: "How oft is the candle of the wicked put out! and how oft cometh their destruction upon them! God distributeth sorrows in his anger. They are as stubble before the wind, and as chaff that the storm carrieth away" (Job 21:17–18). He knew that as well as his friends did, but Job adds to his description of the judgment of the wicked several truths that his friends did not know or had forgotten.

The first great truth Job sets forth is the truth that the wicked often prosper in their wickedness. He says:

7. Wherefore do the wicked live, become old, yea, are mighty in power?
8. Their seed is established in their sight with them, and their offspring before their eyes.
9. Their houses are safe from fear, neither is the rod of God upon them.
10. Their bull gendereth, and faileth not; their cow calveth, and casteth not her calf.
11. They send forth their little ones like a flock, and their children dance.
12. They take the timbrel and harp, and rejoice at the sound of the organ. (21:7–12)

Unlike Asaph in Psalm 73, Job was not troubled by the wicked's present prosperity. He understands that they are under the judgment of God: "They spend their days in wealth, and in a moment go down to the grave" (Job 21:13).

Job speaks of the present prosperity of the wicked because his friends equated earthly prosperity with God's blessing and counted him among those who were without God's blessing—among the wicked—because his prosperity was gone. They made the same mistake that many make today, thinking that because they suffer, God must be punishing them, though they have been faithful to him and to his word. They look at the suffering of others and draw the same conclusion. Job points this out in verses 27–28: "Behold, I know your thoughts, and the devices which ye wrongfully imagine against me. For ye say, Where is the house of the prince? and where are the dwelling places of the wicked?" He means that they saw in his ruined condition proof that he was among the wicked and in so doing imagined wrong against him.

But Job points out a second great truth: that even among the wicked, it is impossible to determine God's attitude toward them from his providential dealings with them. His ways, in that respect, are not equal: "One dieth in his full strength, being wholly at ease and quiet. His breasts are full of milk, and his bones are moistened with marrow. And another dieth in the bitterness of his soul, and never eateth with pleasure" (21:23–25). Yet both are under the judgment of God: "They shall lie down alike in the dust, and the worms shall cover them" (v. 26).

Job is saying that in prosperity or poverty the wicked remain under the judgment of God. There is no happy resurrection for them that will bring them into God's presence forever, as there is for God's people:

29. Have ye not asked them that go by the way? and do ye not know their tokens,
30. That the wicked is reserved to the day of destruction? they shall be brought forth to the day of wrath.
31. Who shall declare his way to his face? and who shall repay him what he hath done?
32. Yet shall he be brought to the grave, and shall remain in the tomb. (21:29–32)

This important truth is denied by those who teach that rain and sunshine, fruitful fields, and health and prosperity represent the blessing of God, that they are a common grace or mercy, a common favor that God shows to the perishing ungodly. It is denied by those who judge the spiritual state of others by their outward circumstances. It is denied by us when we, under trials, think that God has forsaken us, doubting his love for us. Any such denial of this truth is the lie of which Job's friends were guilty (21:34). Job's point is that even as the state of the wicked before God cannot be judged by their outward circumstances, no more can the state of the righteous be so judged. In their misunderstanding of the inscrutability of God's ways, the three friends entirely misjudged Job.

Thus Job comes another step on the way to the resolution of his difficulties. It will take an appearance of God himself to bring about a complete resolution. He was assured of his righteousness before God, not by his works but by the works of his redeemer. He knew that his redeemer lived and that he would see an end to his troubles when he was raised with his redeemer. He understood that God's ways are not our ways, that the wicked often prosper and the righteous often suffer. He had only yet to learn to say, "If all this is true, then there is no point or reason or right in my continuing to ask God to explain his ways to me." That he would learn from Elihu and from God.

Part Four

THE THIRD ROUND
OF SPEECHES

19

THE THIRD SPEECH OF ELIPHAZ

(Job 22)

In Eliphaz's third and last speech it is evident that Job's friends are having difficulty answering him. Zophar does not even speak a third time, and Eliphaz goes fishing for charges of sin to bring against Job.

Eliphaz dismisses Job's attempts to defend himself as a denial of justification by faith alone. What he says is, once again, true in itself.

2. Can a man be profitable unto God, as he that is wise may be profitable unto himself?
3. Is it any pleasure to the Almighty, that thou art righteous? or is it gain to him, that thou makest thy ways perfect?
4. Will he reprove thee for fear of thee? will he enter with thee into judgment? (Job 22:2–4)

The answer to all of these questions is clearly no. God's people knew already then that our works are of no profit to God, that our standing with God does not in any way depend on our works. Applied to Job, the words of Eliphaz amount to a charge of works-righteousness. He means that Job, in defending himself, has attempted to establish his righteousness with God by his own works.

He also turns Job's pleading with God on its head. Job had pleaded with God for an explanation of what had happened to him, and now Eliphaz uses what Job had said as though Job were pleading with God to remember his good works, count him righteous on the basis of those works, and deliver him from his troubles. Having charged Job with works-righteousness, Eliphaz in the same breath charges Job with a lack of good works.

The worst of Eliphaz's charges again Job are found in verses 5–9:

5. Is not thy wickedness great? and thine iniquities infinite?
6. For thou hast taken a pledge from thy brother for nought, and stripped the naked of their clothing.
7. Thou hast not given water to the weary to drink, and thou hast withholden bread from the hungry.
8. But as for the mighty man, he had the earth; and the honourable man dwelt in it.
9. Thou hast sent widows away empty, and the arms of the fatherless have been broken.

Eliphaz is saying that Job misused the wealth God had given him by hoarding it all to himself and not using it to help the poor and needy. Trying to justify himself by his good works, Job actually lacked those good works that were most acceptable to God, or so Eliphaz says. Job was guilty of works-righteousness and hypocrisy.

Eliphaz is right in that hoarding one's gain and wealth and not giving to the widows and orphans and needy is misuse of God's gifts, for what we have is never really ours, but remains God's. He is the sovereign owner of all things, and we are only stewards of what he gives. We show that when we give freely of our abundance to those who are needy. The Heidelberg Catechism reminds us of this in its explanation of the fourth commandment:

> Question 103. What doth God require in the fourth commandment?
>
> Answer. First, that the ministry of the gospel and the schools be maintained; and that I, especially on the sabbath, that is, on the day of rest, diligently frequent the church of God, to hear his word, to use the sacraments, publicly to call upon the Lord, and contribute to the relief of the poor, as becomes a Christian.

It does so again in its explanation of the eighth commandment:

> Question 111. But what doth God require in this commandment?
>
> Answer. That I promote the advantage of my neighbor in every instance I can or may, and deal with him as I desire to be dealt with by others; further also that I faithfully labor, so that I may be able to relieve the needy.[1]

Job, however, was not guilty of these sins. He pleads his innocence of Eliphaz's charges in the following chapters, but Job's friends already knew better. They could not have been ignorant of his reputation when even hell itself was aware of it.

---

1 Heidelberg Catechism Q&A 103, 111, in *Confessions and Church Order*, 128, 132.

Their charges were wicked, not only because they charged Job with great evil—evil of which he was not guilty—but because they offered no proof, did not believe Job's denials of evildoing, and conveniently forgot Job's good reputation. To destroy someone's reputation is a kind of murder, and suspecting evil without proof is the proper work of the devil. No wonder Job later had to offer sacrifice for his friends.

Eliphaz goes on heedlessly to charge Job with thinking that his sins were hid from God. Job, he says, was guilty of spiritual blindness:

10. Therefore snares are round about thee, and sudden fear troubleth thee;
11. Or darkness, that thou canst not see; and abundance of waters cover thee.
12. Is not God in the height of heaven? and behold the height of the stars, how high they are! 13. And thou sayest, How doth God know? can he judge through the dark cloud?
14. Thick clouds are a covering to him, that he seeth not; and he walketh in the circuit of heaven. (Job 22:10–14)

Eliphaz finishes his discourse by reasserting the error that lay at the heart of his charges against Job and that the other two friends had also adopted, the error of believing that prosperity represents God's blessing and trouble his curse and displeasure, an always-popular error. Job had refuted this error in his previous response to Zophar, but Eliphaz gives no heed to what Job had said. He was the one guilty of spiritual blindness.

Eliphaz is running out of words, though, and this will be his last effort. Having gone so far as to charge Job falsely with gross sin, he can go no further. He has allied himself, however unwittingly, with the great slanderer himself and taken Satan's side against Job.

20

JOB'S RESPONSE TO ELIPHAZ

(Job 23–24)

Job's response to Eliphaz really ignores Eliphaz altogether. Insofar as Job pays any attention to what Eliphaz has said, he pleads his case to God, not Eliphaz. When he does address Eliphaz's charges—which he does not even bother with until chapter 24—Job insists that he is not guilty of the sins with which he is charged, and he affirms that God punishes the wicked, but in his own time and often after first raising them up.

In chapter 24, Job brushes aside the words of Eliphaz with disdain. He says that the wicked commit the sins that he has been accused of committing, oppressing the needy and the fatherless, and they do so like beasts, like wild asses, who know not the days of the Almighty, the days in which he judges and punishes wickedness. Nevertheless, both in this life and in death God does punish them—in his own time and place. That is the point of verse 12: "yet God layeth not folly to them." The wicked think they are safe from the judgment of God because he does not immediately punish them, and they rest in that confidence, but God does see: "Though it be given him to be in safety, whereon he resteth; yet his eyes are upon their ways" (v. 23). For the most part they prosper in their wickedness:

4. For there are no bands in their death: but their strength is firm.
5. They are not in trouble as other men; neither are they plagued like other men.
6. Therefore pride compasseth them about as a chain; violence covereth them as a garment.
7. Their eyes stand out with fatness: they have more than heart could wish.
8. They are corrupt, and speak wickedly concerning oppression: they speak loftily.
9. They set their mouth against the heavens, and their tongue walketh through the earth. (Ps. 73:4–9)

Though it may not seem so from a distance as they wallow in their prosperity, God does punish them in this life with terrors: "For the morning is to them even as the shadow of death: if one know them, they are in the terrors of the shadow of death" (Job 24:17). God also punishes them in this life when "their portion is cursed in the earth" (v. 18), an early statement of what Solomon says in Proverbs 3:33. In cursing them, God is not slow to act against them, but is "swift as the waters" (Job 24:18). Nevertheless, that curse of God is not evident, and it is only in the death of the ungodly that their judgment is plain: "They are exalted for a little while, but are gone and brought low; they are taken out of the way as all other, and cut off as the tops of the ears of corn" (v. 24).

All that is immaterial to Job's complaint, however. In chapter 23

Job continues to insist that God owes him an explanation of what had happened to him. His confidence in Christ, his redeemer, has not yet silenced him on that point:

2. Even to day is my complaint bitter: my stroke is heavier than my groaning.
3. Oh that I knew where I might find him! that I might come even to his seat!
4. I would order my cause before him, and fill my mouth with arguments.
5. I would know the words which he would answer me, and understand what he would say unto me. (vv. 2–5)

Job is so foolish as to think that he will find help and comfort in having God answer his insistent "Why?" He does not expect God to justify himself but foolishly thinks that if God will only explain, then he, Job, will be strengthened: "Will he plead against me with his great power? No; but he would put strength in me" (23:6).

Yet when he raises his complaint, God seems far away, seems to have hidden himself: "Behold, I go forward, but he is not there; and backward, but I cannot perceive him: on the left hand, where he doth work, but I cannot behold him: he hideth himself on the right hand, that I cannot see him" (23:8–9). Job even pleads his righteousness as a reason for God to answer his complaint in verses 10–14 and is all the more troubled when there continues to be no response from God (v. 15).

Job does not understand that God owes no one an explanation of his ways. This is the great lesson of his trials. Indeed, to expect an explanation is an offence against the majesty and sovereignty of God: "Nay but, O man, who art thou that repliest against God? Shall the thing formed say to him that formed it, Why hast thou made me thus?" (Rom. 9:20). The context is different in Romans, but the word of God there is apropos to Job's situation and to all God's ways with us.

That God uses our trials and suffering for good we must understand: "When he hath tried me, I shall come forth as gold" (Job 23:10). We may not go any further. To ask why is to set ourselves on the throne of God and call him to account as though he is nothing more than a cringing menial in relation to us. It is a denial of his lordship and absolute sovereignty. When finally we do understand, then we will do as Job did: we will put our hand on our mouth and be silent.

Not only is questioning a denial of God's sovereignty, but it is a denial of salvation by grace alone. We have no works, no merit, that earn for us an answer to our questions. Our standing with God is all through the righteousness of Jesus Christ, and in him alone we must rest.

We, too, when we question God's ways and think we cannot be at peace unless he explains himself to us, will find him a God who hides himself. He is there always to sympathize, to help, to soothe, but he will not be there to stand prisoner at the bar of our questions and to be judged by us. When we are discontented, questioning, doubting, then we will experience what Job did: "Behold, I go forward, but he is not there; and backward, but I cannot perceive him: on the left hand, where he doth work, but I cannot behold him: he hideth himself on the right hand, that I cannot see him" (23:8–9).

Nor would there be any comfort in knowing the rationale of his ways. What we sing in Psalter 211:3 is to the point, especially the third and fourth lines:

Thy way was in the sea, O God,
Thro[ugh] mighty waters, deep and broad,

None understood but God alone,
To man Thy footsteps were unknown;
But safe Thy people Thou didst keep,
Almighty Shepherd of Thy sheep.[1]

Our only comfort in life and in death is that we belong to our Shepherd and Savior.

---

1   No. 211:3 in *The Psalter*.

21

THE THIRD SPEECH
OF BILDAD

(Job 25)

The third speech of Bildad, the last of the speeches of Job's three friends, is pathetic and little more than, "But, but, but, Job, you know that we have no righteousness of our own before God," something Job has himself stated in no uncertain words. That was not the issue, and Bildad's words soon cease. He and his companions are finally silenced.

The content of Bildad's speech is once again doctrinally correct but misapplied to Job. Bildad still thinks that Job is unrighteous before God and guilty of gross sin. His defense of God's righteousness is masterful: "How then can man be justified with God? or how can he be clean that is born of a woman? Behold even to the moon, and it shineth not; yea, the stars are not pure in his sight. How much less man, that is a worm? and the son of man, which is a worm?" (Job 25:4–6). Yet Bildad still believes that Job is attempting to justify himself by his works. He has not even listened to what Job has said.

Bildad makes a great confession of God's sovereignty when he says, "Dominion and fear are with him, he maketh peace in his high places. Is there any number of his armies? and upon whom doth not his light arise?" (25:2–3). He means in his reference to the high places that God sovereignly directs all things to his own purpose, so that they work together in perfect harmony or peace. His armies, as Bildad says, are without number, for all things heavenly and earthly serve him and march to his command and purpose.

Yet Bildad continues to wrong Job. He has no answer to what Job has said but maintains his case against Job. As is so often the case with us, Bildad will not see his error until God himself points it out.

22

JOB'S RESPONSE
TO BILDAD

(Job 26)

Job confesses the inscrutability and incomprehensibility of God in his response to Bildad. His words are a believing echo of what God himself will say to Job when he finally speaks. Job speaks of God's works in the creation (Job 26:5–13) and confesses that what we see of God's power and majesty in the things that are made are but the outskirts of his ways. It is impossible to understand him fully. Job confesses, though in different words, what we find in Romans 11:33–36:

> 33. O the depth of the riches both of the wisdom and knowledge of God! how unsearchable are his judgments, and his ways past finding out!
>
> 34. For who hath known the mind of the Lord? or who hath been his counsellor?
>
> 35. Or who hath first given to him, and it shall be recompensed unto him again?

36. For of him, and through him, and to him, are all
things: to whom be glory for ever. Amen.

The irony of Job's words is that he is answering his own questionings without even realizing it. What he says is the substance
first of Elihu's speech and then of God's, both yet unheard. Yet he
does not take his own words to heart and realize that even if God
did explain himself, Job would not understand. Nor does he apply
to himself the truth that because God is so great it is wrong to
demand an accounting from him.

How like us Job is! We confess the truth with our mouths and
do not apply it to ourselves. We say one thing and think another. We
question and struggle when the answer lies under our noses. Slow of
heart to believe, we find ourselves as troubled as Job. It is only when
God speaks with his almighty power that we finally get it.

Job 26:2-4 is a rebuke. Job rebukes Bildad for his wretched
and insulting attempts to comfort Job, and in rebuking Bildad, he
rebukes all his friends:

2. How hast thou helped him that is without power? how
savest thou the arm that hath no strength?
3. How hast thou counselled him that hath no wisdom?
and how hast thou plentifully declared the thing as it is?
4. To whom hast thou uttered words? and whose spirit
came from thee?

Especially the reference to the Spirit is telling, for Job is saying
to Bildad and the others that their remarks were without the Spirit
of God. All their words were without power, they had no saving
value, they lacked wisdom and counsel, were lies, and must have
been without the Spirit of God. Nevertheless, in condemning his
friends, Job condemns himself, for his complaints and questionings
were as lacking in wisdom, good counsel, and power as their words.

23

JOB'S FINAL SPEECH

(Job 27–31)

In chapters 27–31 Job sums up all that he has said both in answer to his friends and in pouring out his complaint before God. Chapters 27 and 28 are addressed to his friends and chapters 29–31 especially to God.

Chapter 27 has two parts. In verses 1–10 Job once more protests his integrity and righteousness. Once more he refuses to admit to his friends' charges of gross sin and insists that he is righteous before God, not on the basis of welldoing, but in Christ. He not only refuses to accept his friends' accusations, but suggests that in making these charges his friends make themselves liable to the judgment of God: "Let mine enemy be as the wicked, and he that riseth up against me as the unrighteous" (v. 7).

The last half of the chapter is a reiteration of his previous assertion that God does judge the wicked, though in his own time: "For what is the hope of the hypocrite, though he hath gained, when

God taketh away his soul? Will God hear his cry when trouble cometh upon him? Will he delight himself in the Almighty? will he always call upon God?" (27:8–10). He admits the principle but once again fails in the application to himself.

Chapter 28 is about wisdom, both the search for wisdom and God as the source of wisdom. The things of the creation can be discerned, "but where shall wisdom be found? and where is the place of understanding?" (v. 12). Answering his own questions, Job says, "Behold, the fear of the LORD, that is wisdom; and to depart from evil is understanding" (v. 28). Job seems to be introducing a new subject into the discussion, but careful attention to the chapter shows that this is no new subject. Wisdom discerns God's hand in all things, acknowledges his unsearchableness, and humbly bows before him. This wisdom had been lacking in his friends' speeches and had been evident, Job means to say, in his own words. He had not departed from the fear of God.

Once again Job fails to see his own error, the folly of calling God to account and of thinking that he needed an explanation of his troubles from God. What Job says of wisdom reminds us of such verses as Proverbs 1:7 and Ecclesiastes 12:13, but his failure to be wise in the matter of questioning God's ways also reminds us of Ecclesiastes 10:1, which says, "Dead flies cause the ointment of the apothecary to send forth a stinking savour: so doth a little folly him that is in reputation for wisdom and honour." Complaining and calling God to account, Job stank like fouled ointment.

In chapters 29 and 30 Job compares his former condition to his present. He speaks of how he had lost everything, wealth and children, but especially the honor and esteem he once enjoyed. It is generally true that people look up to the rich and honor them, while despising the poor, but Job has reference to his friends. They were the younger who had him in derision. They had made Job their byword (30:9); they had spit in his face (v. 10) and pursued his soul (v. 15).

But Job's complaint is more to God than to them, so we find him describing former days as though even his relationship to God had now changed; he mourns the days "when his candle shined upon my head, and when by his light I walked through darkness; as I was in the days of my youth, when the secret of God was upon my tabernacle; when the Almighty was yet with me" (29:3–5). That was impossible. God's relationship to his people does not change, but God's refusal to answer his questioning made it seem so: "I cry unto thee, and thou dost not hear me: I stand up, and thou regardest me not" (30:20).

In chapter 31 Job returns to his complaint. He insists again, this time before God, that great sin cannot possibly be the reason for his troubles. He mentions his purity of life, the charity he had shown his servants, and the mercy he had shown to the poor as proof that he had lived a life above reproach, as every child of God ought to do. Finding no reason for his troubles in a life of sin, he seeks an explanation from God, forgetting what he himself had said to his friends about the mystery of God's ways.

Nearly every possible sin he might have committed he lists and rejects as the cause of his troubles. He confesses that adultery (even with the eyes), oppression of the poor, and mistreatment of servants and employees are grievous sins and worthy of punishment both by the magistrates and by God. He had not been guilty of sins of the heart, gross covetousness, enmity, hiding his sin, or living in the fear of men. Job does not say he had lived a sinless life. He had already acknowledged his need for a redeemer. He is only saying that gross, unconfessed, presumptuous sin could not be the reason for his sad condition. Since he was not guilty of such sins, his questions are: "Why does it seem as though God is punishing me?" and, "Why will not God hear me when I ask him for a reason?"

In this Job sins grievously. Never may we plead our obedience as a reason for God to answer us. Never may we speak as though our good works cancel out our sinfulness, so that we are not in need of God's chastisement. It was true that Job was upright in his life—God himself had said so to Satan—but our sinfulness is in itself sufficient reason for whatever trials and tribulations God sends us. Job is justifying himself, rather than God, as Elihu points out in the next chapter.

Thus the speeches of Job and his friends come to an unsatisfactory end. His friends are silenced, but Job is still troubled by God's lack of response. The difficulty of reconciling God's love and the suffering of his people has not been resolved. Both Job and his friends have sinned and have not seen their fault. God's justice and sovereignty have been challenged, and the challenge has not been answered. It remains for Elihu and God to speak and to bring all the discussion to a proper, God-glorifying, and comforting conclusion.

Part Five

ELIHU'S ENTRY

24

ELIHU

Job having finished speaking (Job 31:40), and his friends having nothing more to say, Elihu speaks up. The Bible does not tell us when he appeared on the scene—Job 2:11 only mentions the other three. Elihu must have overheard most of the conversation between Job and his friends to be able to judge so truly in the matter, but whether he was there before the other three arrived or came later we do not know.

All we know of Elihu himself is found in chapter 32:2, where he is described as "the son of Barachel the Buzite, of the kindred of Ram." Barachel is not elsewhere mentioned in the Bible, but Buz was a nephew of Abraham. Aram or Ram was the son of Buz's brother Kemuel (Gen. 22:21) or the son of Shem mentioned in Genesis 10:23. In either case, Elihu would be a descendant of Shem and a distant relative of Abraham, still living in the east, the land of Abraham's nativity.

Some would argue that there is no proof that the Buz of Genesis 22 and the Buz of Job 32 are the same, but the evidence is compelling. Not only are the names, Buz and Ram, found together (Genesis 10:23 also mentions a son of Aram named Uz), but these are the only two places in the Bible where these names are found. Letting scripture itself guide us therefore, we can come to no other conclusion but that Elihu was a Semite, related to Abraham, and that the book of Job dates to those days of Abraham.

This means that the knowledge of God, of spiritual things, of the resurrection of the dead, of the Messiah himself, were not later developments but common knowledge already in the earliest times. Only those who deny the divine inspiration of the Bible deny this, denying that God revealed himself as the God and Savior of his people from the beginning. The Heidelberg Catechism notes this early knowledge of God, the Savior, in answer 19 when it speaks of the gospel: "which God himself first revealed in Paradise; and afterwards published by the patriarchs and prophets, and represented by the sacrifices and other ceremonies of the law; and lastly, has fulfilled it by his only begotten Son."[1]

The only other thing we know of Elihu is that he was younger than the others and for that reason did not speak until he had heard them out: "And Elihu the son of Barachel the Buzite answered and said, I am young, and ye are very old; wherefore I was afraid, and durst not shew you mine opinion. I said, Days should speak, and multitude of years should teach wisdom" (Job 32:6–7). Having heard them out and heard no wisdom from them, he is impelled to speak.

The Bible, as always, has so little to say of Elihu personally because it is his words, not his personal details, that matter. Unlike the others, what Elihu has to say is not only factually true, but the truth as both Job and his friends needed to hear it. When Elihu is finished speaking, God repeats much of what Elihu says.

---

1   Heidelberg Catechism A 19, in *Confessions and Church Order*, 89.

25

ELIHU'S SPEECH

(Job 32–37)

Because most of what Elihu says is directed to Job, there are those who think that Elihu takes the side of Job's three friends and continues their arguments against him. Chapter 32:3 shows that this is not the case; Elihu was angry with Job, but he was also angry with the three friends "because they had found no answer, and yet had condemned Job." Nor is the content of Elihu's speech an echo of theirs. What they had said was true but misapplied to Job. God would finish the argument against Job and bring him to his knees, but what Elihu says is true and the first part of what Job needed to hear.

In the middle of his speech Elihu pauses and invites Job to speak: "If thou hast any thing to say, answer me: speak, for I desire to justify thee" (Job 33:32), but Job is silent, acknowledging the truth of Elihu's words. He does not speak again except to humble himself before God. When Elihu says, "I desire to justify thee," he does not mean he is pleading Job's case, but rather giving Job opportunity to argue his case with Elihu as he did with the other three.

That Elihu chastises Job so severely and chastises him almost exclusively may seem unfair on Elihu's part. We must remember, though, that the three friends had sinned against Job, but Job against God. They were guilty of breaking the ninth commandment, which is sin against God, but Job's words were a violation of the third commandment—their words were aimed at Job, but Job's were aimed at God. Elihu, then, is correct when he says of Job, "For he addeth rebellion unto his sin, he clappeth his hands among us, and multiplieth his words against God" (34:37).

Elihu's part in speaking is to chastise Job for his errors and sins, and it is notable that God adds nothing more to what Elihu says of Job's sins. Perhaps God's own rebuke would have been too much for Job, and God who remembers "that we are dust" (Ps. 103:14) mercifully leaves that to one of Job's equals. God shows, even before Job humbles himself in God's presence, that all is already forgiven, that he has already put Job's sins behind his back.

God displays this same mercy to us in sending others to point out our sins and not hailing us into his own presence to deal with them there. With whatever weaknesses others come to show us what we have done wrong, it is still God's mercy and not something to be rejected as an act of pride on their part. Far better them than the august face of God! Not until the judgment day will we have to give an account to him, and then only as those whose sins are already forgiven and who stand in the shadow of Christ through whom God judges. Only with souls and bodies redeemed and cleansed of all sin and unrighteousness will we stand in his presence to be judged.

Besides chastising Job, it is Elihu's part to remind Job of what he already knew, that chastisement is grace, not judgment. Job had to remember to sing:

O righteous God, Thy chastisement,
Though sent through foes, in love is sent;
Though grievous, it will profit me,
A healing ointment it shall be. (Psalter 386:5; Psalm 141)[1]

Because Job had offended the majesty and sovereignty of God in calling God to account and demanding an explanation of his ways, God could not deal with Job as an equal in speaking of the gracious purpose of chastisement but sends Elihu, Job's equal, as his messenger.

Elihu's principle charge against Job is that "he justified himself rather than God" (Job 32:2). This cannot mean that Job tried to justify himself by works rather than by faith. Job's admissions of his own sinfulness and his trust in Christ as redeemer (19:24–27) prove otherwise. Even in insisting that he was not guilty of the gross sins with which his friends charged him, Job did not make his integrity his righteousness before God. God testified, too, to Job's integrity (1:8), something he would not have done if Job was trusting in his own works.

Elihu is referring to Job's complaints and pleas. By insisting that God owed him an explanation and that he could not rest until God gave him one, Job put his own imagined right to an answer before God's sovereign right to act as he wills, when and where he will, without ever having to give an account of himself to his creatures. What Job should have said, though it is beyond saying without God's all-sufficient grace, is what Eli said: "It is the LORD: let him do what seemeth him good" (1 Sam. 3:18).

Such a lesson for us! We may not presume to hold back or stay God's hand by thinking that he may do nothing unless he explains

---

1 No. 386:5, in *The Psalter*.

himself to us, though we may be tempted to do so in adversity. We may not complain or question his ways and so say to him, "What doest thou?" Shall the clay speak so to the potter? Such presumption is far greater sin than the horrifying slander of Job's friends.

Elihu begins by pleading his youth, his inexperience, his fear as the reason for his previous silence. He waited for the others to finish because he thought that "days should speak, and multitude of years should teach wisdom" (Job 32:7). To their shame the three friends had proved the contrary: "Great men are not always wise: neither do the aged understand judgment" (v. 9). Confessing then that wisdom is the gift of God, Elihu takes it upon himself to speak: "But there is a spirit in man: and the inspiration of the Almighty giveth them understanding" (v. 8). Nor could Elihu keep silence because the honor and glory of God were at stake.

Though he pleads his youth and lack of wisdom, Elihu lays down the fundamental principle that both Job and his friends had missed in all their talking: "God thrusteth [Job] down, not man" (32:13). To Job he is saying what Paul says in Romans 9:20: "Nay but, O man, who art thou that repliest against God?" To the three friends it is a sharp rebuke of their efforts in thrusting Job down further than God had thrust him and a reminder that they had pushed themselves into the place of God by presuming to judge Job. This is the theme that God takes up when he reveals himself in the whirlwind.

Instead of following up on that point, Elihu leaves it to God to speak on behalf of his own glory and honor. Elihu instead turns to the subject of God's gracious purpose in chastisement:

16. Then he openeth the ears of men, and sealeth their instruction,
17. That he may withdraw man from his purpose, and hide pride from man.

18. He keepeth back his soul from the pit, and his life from perishing by the sword....
25. His flesh shall be fresher than a child's: he shall return to the days of his youth:
26. He shall pray unto God, and he will be favourable unto him: and he shall see his face with joy: for he will render unto man his righteousness.
27. He looketh upon men, and if any say, I have sinned, and perverted that which was right, and it profited me not;
28. He will deliver his soul from going into the pit, and his life shall see the light.
29. Lo, all these things worketh God oftentimes with man,
30. To bring back his soul from the pit, to be enlightened with the light of the living. (Job 33:16–18, 25–30)

Elihu is speaking of God's word, his self-revelation. In those days he gave his word directly: "For God speaketh once, yea twice, yet man perceiveth it not. In a dream, in a vision of the night, when deep sleep falleth upon men, in slumberings upon the bed; then he openeth the ears of men, and sealeth their instruction" (33:14–16). Job had that word of God passed down from father to son and so did his friends. That word is designed to keep men's souls from the pit, but because men never heed his word as they should, because they are dull of hearing, then, as it pleases him, he sends chastisement:

19. He is chastened also with pain upon his bed, and the multitude of his bones with strong pain:
20. So that his life abhorreth bread, and his soul dainty meat.
21. His flesh is consumed away, that it cannot be seen; and his bones that were not seen stick out.

22. Yea, his soul draweth near unto the grave, and his life
to the destroyers. (vv. 19–22)

When sending chastisement, God sends others, his messengers
(Elihu was one of them), to remind men of his gracious purpose
in chastisement: "If there be a messenger with him, an interpreter,
one among a thousand, to shew unto man his uprightness: then he
is gracious unto him, and saith, Deliver him from going down to
the pit: I have found a ransom" (33:23–24). God sends such today
when he sends those who preach the gospel. He sends them to
speak of the ransom God has found for his people and to show
that because this ransom has been paid, God cannot and will not
be other than gracious even when he afflicts.

It is at this point that Elihu pauses and challenges Job to reply,
but Job has nothing to say for Elihu speaks truth and speaks to Job's
heart. When God's ransom in Christ is preached to the believing
heart, there can be no longer any complaint or dissatisfaction with
God's ways. Then all the troubles of life become but a "light affliction" in comparison, and we see that they must work "for us a far
more exceeding and eternal weight of glory" (2 Cor. 4:17). Job had
looked too much at the things that are seen, but Elihu turns his
attention once again to those things that are unseen and eternal,
and seeing them, Job is rendered speechless.

Having been used by God to silence Job, Elihu turns in chapters 34 and 35 to some of Job's foolish utterances and corrects
them, also for the benefit of Job's friends: "Hear my words, O ye
wise men; and give ear unto me, ye that have knowledge. For the
ear trieth words, as the mouth tasteth meat. Let us choose to us
judgment: let us know among ourselves what is good. For Job hath
said I am righteous: and God hath taken away my judgment" (Job
34:2–5; compare Job 27).

This, Elihu reminds him, is the speech of wicked men: "What man is like Job, who drinketh up scorning like water? Which goeth in company with the workers of iniquity, and walketh with wicked men" (34:7–8). Elihu does not refer to the scorning that Job endured but to his scorning of God by questioning the justice and judgment of God. Job sinned grievously: "He addeth rebellion unto his sin, he clappeth his hands among us, and multiplieth his words against God" (v. 37).

Elihu's answer to Job's words and to the words of Job's friends is simply, "Therefore hearken unto me, ye men of understanding: far be it from God, that he should do wickedness; and from the Almighty, that he should commit iniquity….Yea, surely God will not do wickedly, neither will the Almighty pervert judgment" (34:10, 12). Elihu elaborates on this in verses 13–30, but the answer is really that God is God, the same answer that Romans 9 gives to this kind of wicked speech. We may not understand his ways, but his ways are always just and right.

What Job ought to have said was, "I have borne chastisement, I will not offend any more: that which I see not teach thou me: if I have done iniquity, I will do no more" (Job 34:31–32), thus acknowledging that there is no one unworthy of chastisement and that in chastising his own, God does according to the good pleasure of his own will. Once again neither Job nor his friends have any response, though Elihu presses them to respond in the final verses of the chapter.

Elihu goes on to correct another misstatement of Job's: "Thinkest thou this to be right, that thou saidst, My righteousness is more than God's? For thou saidst, What advantage will it be unto thee? and, What profit shall I have, if I be cleansed from my sin?" (35:2–3; compare 9:30–31; 21:15). Job, in demanding an account from God, had set himself up as God's judge, as though his righteousness were more than God's and as though it would add something to God. In complaining that there is no profit in righteousness he had denied God's sovereignty.

Elihu does not bother to plead that God does bless obedience in his own time and in his own way. He does not plead our calling to serve God even if he slay us. He turns the tables on Job and says in effect, "You say that there should be profit for you in serving God, that at the very least he should explain himself to you? The truth is that our obedience doesn't profit him at all nor our disobedience hurt him. God is so great and so far above us that even to speak of profiting in his presence is vanity."

To put it another way, to speak of meriting, earning, profiting, deserving with God, of having any rights before him or any credit with him, is to forget his independence of anything or anyone. It is to forget that we are but his creatures who belong to him so entirely that we do not deserve even his thanks (Luke 17:7–10). What Job had said was vanity and "without knowledge" of God (Job 35:16). What Job should have done was trust God, not question him (v. 14), for faith is all that is left to the poor sinner who stands in the presence of God, and even that he has not except God give it.

There are other statements of Job spoken in haste and without thought, but enough is enough, and neither Elihu nor God chide further. Elihu turns instead and again to the wonderful truth that God has his own gracious purpose in chastisement, and that in contrast to his dealings with the "hypocrites in heart" who "heap up wrath" (36:13). What a comfort to know that "he withdraweth not his eyes from the righteous" (v. 7).

Elihu speaks of the righteous being enthroned (36:7), of deliverance from affliction (v. 15), of prosperity and pleasure (v. 11). In light of all Elihu has said, however, he is not changing his tune and telling Job that there is after all the possibility of profiting with God—that serving God will bring health, wealth, and earthly peace. The words of chapter 36:7 are the key to all Elihu says: "Yea, he doth establish them [the righteous] for ever, and they are exalted." There is a reward to the righteous, in this life peace with God and the blessedness of knowing God, and in the end eternal prosperity and blessedness, but that reward is also grace.

Yet the matter is not finished. Elihu's closing words concerning the majesty and greatness of God are but the stage from which God will reveal his glory to Job, humbling him, silencing him, teaching him, and showing mercy to him.

Green sums up Elihu's speech thus:

Elihu has now fulfilled the task assigned to him. He was charged with removing misapprehensions from Job's mind and correcting the mistakes into which he had fallen. But it was not given to him to extricate Job entirely out of Satan's snare and accomplish for him the full and blessed effects of his temptation. This work the LORD reserved for Himself, to be performed in His own person. Elihu is but His messenger sent before His face to prepare His way before Him. And now even while he is speaking the rumbling is heard of distant thunder (37:2); heavy masses of cloud begin to darken the sky, and the advancing tempest betokens the LORD's approach. Elihu points to these insignia of the divine Majesty as they steadily draw near, and his own voice is hushed in awe. All are mute in solemn expectation. It is the LORD who comes.[2]

---

2   Green, *The Argument of the Book of Job Unfolded*, 280–81.

Part Six

GOD AND JOB

26

GOD'S REVELATION
OF HIMSELF
TO JOB

(Job 38–39)

While Elihu is still speaking to Job, God draws near in a storm, and even Elihu can think of little else but the awesome presence of God and soon falls silent:

32. With clouds he covereth the light; and commandeth it not to shine by the cloud that cometh betwixt.
33. The noise thereof sheweth concerning it, the cattle also concerning the vapour.

1. At this also my heart trembleth, and is moved out of his place.
2. Hear attentively the noise of his voice, and the sound that goeth out of his mouth.
3. He directeth it under the whole heaven, and his lightning unto the ends of the earth.

4. After it a voice roareth: he thundereth with the voice of his excellency; and he will not stay them when his voice is heard.

5. God thundereth marvellously with his voice; great things doeth he, which we cannot comprehend. (Job 36:32–33; 37:1–5)

Scripture often associates storms with the majesty and coming of God. Psalm 18:7–13 is a good example, as versified in the Psalter:

4. He came: the earth's foundations quake,
   The hills are shaken from their place,
   Thick smoke and fire devouring break
   In anger dread before His face.

5. Descending through the bending skies,
   With gloom and darkness under Him,
   Forth through the storm Jehovah flies
   As on the wings of cherubim.

6. Thick darkness hides Him from the view,
   And swelling clouds His presence veil,
   Until His glorious light breaks through
   In lightning flash and glistening hail.

7. Jehovah's thunders fill the heaven,
   The dreadful voice of God Most High;
   With shafts of light the clouds are riven,
   His foes, dismayed, in terror fly.

8. The raging torrents overflow,
   And sweep the world's foundations bare,
   Because Thy blasts of anger blow,
   O Lord of earth and sea and air.[1]

---

1 No. 34: 4–8, in *The Psalter.*

At Sinai, in the wilderness, in the pillar of cloud and fire, in his coming with clouds at the end of all things, the power and ferocity of storms announce his presence both as judge and as savior of his people. In this case he comes as savior of Job and his three friends.

From the storm God speaks, and if the storm were not enough to silence every mouth, God holds before his servant Job his unspeakable and incomprehensible glory as creator and upholder of all things. He does so in language that is unparalleled in the rest of scripture, in language that leaves no doubt as to the origin and existence of all things visible and invisible. This is the meeting with God that Job had desired, but how different in reality from anything Job imagined.

He had said, "O that one might plead for a man with God, as a man pleadeth for his neighbour!" (Job 16:21), and, "Oh that I knew where I might find him! that I might come even to his seat! I would order my cause before him, and fill my mouth with arguments. I would know the words which he would answer me, and understand what he would say unto me" (23:3–5). Getting what he wished, Job finds he has nothing to say. When God reveals himself to Job in thunder, speaking of his mighty works, Job finds that God is more than a neighbor.

God speaks to Job of things great and small, near and far, earthly and heavenly and otherworldly, of things we think we know and of things that all the efforts of science have still not puzzled out. He speaks of his work as creator and ruler of all things, but also of his sovereignty over hell and over the hearts of men. He speaks of beasts and of angels. Some things of which God speaks we can name ourselves, but there are things of which God speaks that leave us wondering, the unicorn and behemoth and leviathan.

It would require an encyclopedia to summarize the knowledge that all the efforts of men and six thousand years of history have gathered of the few things of which God speaks. Yet all the knowledge men have gained leaves mankind merely poking at the edges of God's works, and they do so without ever seeing God's handiwork in the things he has made. Job had confessed earlier, "Lo, these are parts of his ways: but how little a portion is heard of him? but the thunder of his power who can understand?" (26:14). So it will always be with man and his investigations.

God's words concerning his work as creator are all designed to teach Job how small he is in relation to God, and so God asks: "Who are you? What do you know? Where were you when I created all things?" God's words not only put Job to shame, but put to shame the folly of those who believe that things exist of themselves and who, by positing billions of years, think they have answered all questions concerning the origin of this universe. They put to shame those who think that they by scientific investigation and experiment or by philosophic argument have ruled God out of existence. They put us to shame also when we think we know anything at all. Solomon, the wisest of all, says, "As thou knowest not what is the way of the spirit, nor how the bones do grow in the womb of her that is with child: even so thou knowest not the works of God who maketh all" (Eccl. 11:5).

Men have begun to explore the depths of the sea (Job 38:16), but they know only a little of what the oceans hold and that without truly understanding what they find. All men die but have not yet been able to define the moment of death (v. 17). All the efforts of science have failed in understanding what light is (vv. 19–20). An examination of the snow shows us the unvarying pattern of every flake, but who can fathom the difference between every flake that has ever fallen on the face of the earth (v. 22)? Science gives us the means to learn about the stars and other wonders of the universe, but God knows their names and number (vv. 31–33).

Man gives his weather reports but can do nothing to change what God has decreed (vv. 25–30).

The mountain goats, the deer, the lion, the raven, the wild goats, the wild asses, the unicorn, the peacock, the ostrich, the horse, the hawk, and the eagle (Job 39) all display God's power and divinity, as do all created things (Rom. 1:20). Yet who is able to explain the migration of the hawk, the folly of the ostrich, the hunting prowess of the lion, the beauty of the peacock? Only the creator of these things knows the why and how of what he has made.

Why does God speak of these things to Job? We expect to read of God's power and wisdom and grace as savior, even of his sovereign right as judge, but instead he speaks of his works as creator and as the God of providence. Why?

We must understand that God did not come to Job to answer his questionings, his "why?" A careful reading of Job 38–41 will show that God gives no explanation at all of Job's trials. He does not tell Job what went on in heaven before Job's troubles began. He never speaks of Satan's part in Job's losses. He does not even repeat what Elihu had said about his gracious purpose in affliction. What Elihu had said was true but was not an explanation of God's ways. Indeed, though Elihu has confessed that "all things work together for good to them that love God" (Rom. 8:28), the question of how they work and why they work for good remains unanswered. God's revelation of himself and his works to Job is God's way of saying to Job, "My thoughts are not your thoughts, neither are your ways my ways" (Isa. 55:8).

Green puts it well:

The fact is, this discourse is not directed to an elucidation of that mystery at all. It is not the design of God to offer a vindication of His dealings with men in general, or a justification of His providence towards Job. He has no intention of placing Himself at the bar of His creatures, and erecting them into judges of His conduct. He is not amenable to them, and He does not recognize their right to be censors of Him and of His ways. The righteousness of His providence does not depend upon their perceiving or admitting it. The Lord does not here stand on the defensive, nor allow it to appear as though He were in any need of being relieved from the strictures of Job, or it were of any account to Him whether feeble worms approved His dealings or confessed the propriety of His dispensations.[2]

Job has already profited from his trials. He has come through them to a stronger faith in his redeemer and to a greater assurance of eternal life. Though unwittingly, he has disproved Satan's slander and proved that God's grace makes friends and lovers of God, not mercenaries. He has by his patience proved the efficacy of God's electing purpose, the cleansing power of the blood of Christ, not yet shed, and the sovereignty and graciousness of the Spirit's work.

Job's piety, his integrity, and his trust in God have been abundantly and unquestionably evident, but God has a further purpose with Job. Job's relationship to God had been set askew by his questions, and his sins had come between him and God. He had to be brought to repentance that that relationship might flourish once again. He had to learn that God is the great redeemer of his people, not in spite of their trials and afflictions, but in their trials

---

2 Green, *The Argument of the Book of Job Unfolded*, 286–87.

and afflictions. All this God shows to Job by the revelation of his incomprehensible works of creation and providence.

Job's questions had been out of place and were sin against God, but God does not want mere stoical submission from Job. He wants from Job a living trust that rests always and in all circumstances in the confidence that God is gracious and good in all his works and ways, though without understanding God's works and ways. That is the point of James 5:11: "Behold, we count them happy which endure. Ye have heard of the patience of Job, and have seen the end of the Lord; that the Lord is very pitiful, and of tender mercy." The "end" of the Lord is his purpose, always merciful and gracious. Job finally saw that "end" of the Lord and saw that God's "end," his purpose, was merciful both in prosperity and in affliction, and so must we.

What a lesson for us who are far behind Job in experiencing God's gracious purpose in affliction! If Job still had to learn these lessons, then where are we in comparison to him, to whom there was not like in all the earth (Job 1:8)? If Job had to suffer such appalling loss to teach him these lessons, then what lies ahead for us? Only God knows, of course, and we must read the story of Job, applying it to ourselves in the confidence that God who has begun a good work in us will finish it as he did with his servant Job.

27

GOD'S REBUKE OF JOB, JOB'S RESPONSE, AND GOD'S CONTINUED SPEECH TO JOB

(Job 40–41)

God pauses in this great doxology of praise to his own glory and invites Job to respond: "Moreover the LORD answered Job, and said, Shall he that contendeth with the Almighty instruct him? he that reproveth God, let him answer it" (Job 40:1–2). He is asking, "Job, do you really want to set yourself up as my judge and the one to whom I must answer? Do you understand now that you have taken it upon yourself to teach me, the God of heaven and earth? What do you have to say for yourself? Surely you understand that you 'must not argue and debate' with me."[1]

Job immediately responds and tells God that he will be silent

---

1   Calvin, *Sermons from Job*, 49.

and will listen to whatever else God has to say to him. When he says, "I am vile" (40:4), he does not refer to his sinfulness but to how he feels in God's presence, small and contemptible. Who would not? Being out in the creation, perhaps on a clear and starry night in the mountains, we sometimes feel as Job did, very small indeed. Reading Job 38–41 is overwhelming, but Job stood in the presence of God and heard the voice of him whose speech moves the planets and the stars and calls them all by name. How insignificant he must have felt!

God is not finished with Job, however, and goes on to speak of two of the mightiest of his creatures, behemoth on land and leviathan in the sea. There is much debate about these creatures. Some say a behemoth is an elephant or hippopotamus and a leviathan a crocodile or whale. Others say they are extinct creatures, perhaps kinds of dinosaurs. Some deny they are real creatures, though scripture seems to be describing such. They say that these are mythical beasts or figures of Satan and refer to Isaiah 27:1, where *leviathan* is a name for Satan, synonymous there with the crooked or piercing serpent, the dragon.

Much of this debate is beside the point. God is telling Job that the greatest of all created things are but the work of his hands, his servants. Whether they symbolize Satan or not makes little difference, for if behemoth and leviathan are God's servants, then so is Satan, whether or not he is the leviathan referred to by God. The message is clear: God is great indeed, greater than all his creatures and answerable to none of them—most certainly not to Job. He is God, the unchangeable creator and savior of his people. Though circumstances change, God does not change, neither as creator nor as the redeemer of his people. If he is Job's redeemer, then he must be that not only in prosperity and health but also in the death of Job's dear children and the loss of his possessions.

Job had said, "What? shall we receive good at the hand of God, and shall we not receive evil?" (Job 2:10). Though he meant nothing wrong, he was learning that there is no evil for God's children but only good, however that good may come—no evil because God is God, incomprehensible but gracious in his dealings with the children of men.

We do not mean that the troubles of life and all the suffering we go through cannot be described as evils. Scripture itself uses that word to describe them (Deut. 31:21; Ps. 40:12). Nevertheless, using that word must not lead us to think, consciously or subconsciously, that God is dealing evilly with us or intends evil. Into that error Job had fallen because God would not answer his "why?" We fall into the same error when we begin to be discouraged, to complain of God's ways, and to repine. Only when we measure the pleasant things of life and the afflictions of life with the standard of God's word and not by the circumstances themselves do we see that good and evil are the same in God's sovereign good pleasure and purpose.

It is not God's purpose in these chapters simply to overwhelm Job with a sense of his majesty and drive him to his knees in submission, but God's speech to Job must be taken along with what Elihu had said. With a voice of thunder, God adds to Elihu's message of gracious goodness the wonderful truth that because he is God, exalted in all his works and ways, grace and goodness are from everlasting to everlasting on those who fear him. Before these truths Job is not only silent but sorrowful, confessing his sin, seeing God's dealing with him in an entirely new light.

This is the end of the Lord mentioned in James 5:11: "Behold, we count them happy which endure. Ye have heard of the patience of Job, and have seen the end of the Lord; that the Lord is very pitiful, and of tender mercy." The word *end* refers to God's purpose and goal in Job's suffering—in this case, Job's growth in grace, stronger faith in his redeemer and in the resurrection of the body, and greater insight into the majesty and greatness of God, a worthy end indeed.

In all of this Job learns to be patient and endure, and so do we. Whatever trials and suffering God sends us—and most of us will never be called to suffer as Job did—we, too, learn patience and endurance. We have the example of Job to help us learn those most difficult lessons and to teach us that in endurance is happiness. That is the counting of which James 5:11 speaks. May we count accurately and well.

God has different purposes in afflicting his people. He sanctifies us, teaches us his glory, makes us depend on him, strengthens our faith, and builds our assurance through trials. Sometimes his purpose is only to prove the sufficiency of his grace. At other times he sends affliction not for our benefit so much as for the strengthening of his cause and kingdom in the world. He afflicts Job as much for our benefit as for Job's. In it all he leads us to the end of which James speaks, proving that he is indeed God alone, but always also "pitiful and of tender mercy," (James 5:11) the God and Father of his people.

28

JOB'S CONFESSION
AND REPENTANCE

(Job 42:1–6)

When God speaks, we can either close our eyes and ears and harden our hearts against him or humble ourselves before him as Job does and as every one of God's children must. Humility before God was purchased at the cross and is given by the Spirit. We cannot do otherwise, then, than be humble in his presence. Yet our humility before God is not the servile groveling of those who have been forced to their knees but the awestruck wonder of those who see in one so great and so entirely beyond our comprehension a Father and a Savior. That is what Job means when he says, "I know that thou canst do every thing" (Job 42:2).

Job is not confessing the mere power of God but saying, "Now I see that thou art able to make all things turn to my advantage, to save me by prosperity and adversity, by health and sickness, by fruitful and barren years, and seeing that, I no longer need to know how and why. I am the clay, thou art the potter. Do unto me as it seems fit unto thee." We sing it in the hymn:

1. Have Thine own way, Lord,
Have Thine own way;
Thou art the Potter,
I am the clay.
Mould me and make me
After Thy will,
While I am waiting,
Yielded and still.

2. Have Thine own way, Lord,
Have Thine own way;
Search me and try me,
Master, today.
Whiter than snow, Lord,
Wash me just now,
As in Thy presence
Humbly I bow.

3. Have Thine own way, Lord,
Have Thine own way;
Wounded and weary,
Help me, I pray.
Power, all power,
Surely is Thine,
Touch me and heal me,
Savior divine.

4. Have Thine own way, Lord,
Have Thine own way;
Hold o'er my being
Absolute sway.
Fill with Thy Spirit
Till all shall see
Christ only, always,
Living in me.[1]

Job's confession is remarkable. Looking back to former days of prosperity and peace, he acknowledges that he did not really know God before all his troubles began: "I have heard of thee by the hearing of the ear: but now mine eye seeth thee" (Job 42:5). Job means that until God appeared in the whirlwind, his knowledge of God had been too much theoretical. He had, as we say, known of God but had not known him personally and experientially as he ought to have done. So it is too often with us. We know what scripture teaches of God, can list his attributes, and speak glowingly of his glory. That knowledge is valuable and is part of faith (2 Tim. 1:12), but it must translate into that knowledge that is eternal life, the knowledge that comes from walking with God and talking

1 "Have Thine Own Way, Lord," Adelaide A. Pollard, accessed September 15, 2020, https://hymnary.org/text/have_thine_own_way_lord.

with him. Such knowledge often comes, as it did for Job, through adversity and trials.

Job confesses his sin in speaking foolishly of and to God. He recognizes that in asking God for an explanation of his providences, he had dared to act as God's counselor and had done so without proper knowledge of God. In speaking of God he had not guarded his "tongue from evil" or his "lips from speaking guile" (Ps. 34:13), but he had "uttered that [he] understood not; things too wonderful for [him], which [he] knew not" (Job 42:3). How important it is in preaching, in witnessing, in speaking of God and of the things of God, to do so praying that God will guard the door of our lips, for there are no sins of the tongue worse than to speak wrongly of him. As Paul writes, "For who hath known the mind of the Lord? or who hath been his counsellor?" (Rom. 11:34).

Job's self-abhorrence is part of his repentance and amounts to this: "I despise myself for doing what I have done, for thinking and saying and doing what dishonors the name and grace of my God." It is the breast-beating of the publican in the temple and the confession that in our own experience we are the chief of sinners, for though we can find excuses for others we can find no excuse for ourselves. Such self-abhorrence is not to be despised, for it was purchased with the blood of God's Son and is ours only through the work of the Spirit of God in our hearts. It may not be despised or spurned when we see it in others who have come to us confessing their sins, and God does not despise it in us. Humbling ourselves before God after the example of Job, we find the truth of Psalm 51:17: "The sacrifices of God are a broken spirit: a broken and a contrite heart, O God, thou wilt not despise." We find that when we humble ourselves in the sight of the Lord, he does lift us up (James 4:10). We find that he gives "grace unto the humble" (v. 6). The lesson we must learn in our trials, then, is simply, "Humble yourselves therefore under the mighty hand of God, that he may exalt you in due time" (1 Pet. 5:6), and by grace we do come always and again to prostrate ourselves in his presence.

When Job says, "Hear, I beseech thee, and I will speak: I will demand of thee, and declare thou unto me" (Job 42:4), he is not still demanding an accounting from God but humbly beseeching God to hear and receive his confession of sin. Though confident of his righteousness, he asks God to declare to him once again his righteousness as he mourns for his sins. We would not even dare to go to God confessing our sins having sinned so often and so grievously if we were not sure of our righteousness, but we need to hear again, when we have sinned, his justifying declaration: "He hath not beheld iniquity in Jacob, neither hath he seen perverseness in Israel: the LORD his God is with him, and the shout of a king is among them" (Num. 23:21). And so we, with Job, come asking, "Tell me again, Lord."

29

GOD'S REBUKE OF JOB'S FRIENDS

(Job 42:7–9)

It is a measure of Job's sin against God that God deals with him first and only then with his three friends. We would count the slanderous words of his friends the greater evil, especially if they had been directed at us, but Job had spoken in a way that did not glorify God. Nevertheless, the sin of his friends had to be shown, and they also brought to repentance. They, too, in speaking against Job, had spoken foolishly against God, and God tells them that he is angry with them, so angry that he would accept only Job's prayers on their behalf (Job 42:8). They, too, had misjudged and spoken against God's dealings with Job, but because they had shown themselves to be among God's children, there was forgiveness for them also.

God addresses Eliphaz as the oldest of the three and therefore the most accountable, for wisdom should belong to those who are of age. He and the other two had to take seven cows and seven rams and offer them as a sacrifice in Job's presence, asking Job to pray for them. God threatens to deal with them according to their folly to impress on them the seriousness of what they had done and their need for atoning sacrifice. Seven and seven surely emphasized to them that this was a matter of fellowship and of covenantal communion with God. Their sins, too, had come between them and God and needed to be taken out of the way.

This they did without argument, and Job, forgiving them, prayed for their forgiveness and reconciliation to God, a demonstration of the great truth that those who are forgiven much are also able to forgive others. Job had much to forgive, but the sins committed by his friends were nothing in comparison to what he had been forgiven by God. The foundation for all this was the multiple sacrifices offered in Job's presence and God's, pointing to the sacrifice of Christ, the only ground for forgiveness.

Certainly some would find this hard to accept. Job is not allowed to harbor any grudge against his friends. His friends are not allowed to excuse themselves with the plea that it was an honest misunderstanding. Job is not allowed to excuse himself with reference to his great losses, nor they by their evident concern for Job and his well-being. Sin must be forgiven and gotten out of the way for there to be fellowship with God and communion with others. May we never forget it.

The most interesting thing in this exchange is the way in which God deals with Job and the friends—not individually, but together. The friends must bring the sacrifices, and on the basis of those sacrifices Job also is accepted by God and his prayer heard. The friends must ask Job to pray for them and must offer the sacrifices in Job's presence, so they are accepted, justified with Job before the great God who had appeared to them. Faith in Christ's sacrifice for sin and sharing in the benefits of his sacrifice also makes us members of one another. Together we find forgiveness, and together we are received by God and blessed.

30

THE CONCLUDING
HISTORY OF JOB

(Job 42:10–17)

Having restored Job spiritually, God also restores his family and fortunes. This, too, God does through family and friends. Each visitor brings money and jewelry, and what is far more important, comfort. Through them Job is in the end twice as wealthy as he was before, and in the 140 years that remain he is blessed with ten more children, seven sons and three daughters. All this raises questions, however.

Does Job's new prosperity equal God's blessing? Is it proof that God loves him and is his God? Green's commentary is largely based on the premise that "goodness and happiness go hand in hand in the ordinary experiences of this world," but Green is wrong.[1] Prosperity does not equal blessing, nor adversity God's disfavor. If that were the case, then all the lies of Job's friends would be true, and

---

1   Green, *The Argument of the Book of Job Unfolded*, 14.

his former misfortune would be proof of God's disfavor and judgment. The whole history of Job proves otherwise.

Earthly prosperity, long life, and good health are not the blessing or grace of God and cannot be interpreted, even in the Old Testament, to be such, not individually. In the Old Testament they did represent God's favor to Israel on a national scale and the opposite his disfavor to Israel on a national scale, but never on a personal level. God's providences could not be and cannot be used as the standard to judge his attitude toward anyone. If we judge God's dealing with others that way, we fall into the error of Job's friends. If we judge God's providences that way in our own lives, we will fall into the error of Job and begin asking for an explanation.

That is, it bears repeating, the error of the false doctrine of common grace: rain and sunshine, fruitful fields, long life, and earthly prosperity are the blessing of God, so it is said. That leaves the ungodly in their prosperity with more grace than the afflicted child of God to whom ill health, drought, failed crops, and an early death are evidence of a lack of grace and favor. One cannot have it both ways. Each believer's trials are as much grace as his peace and prosperity, and for the ungodly, prosperity is as much a curse as the troubles he experiences. His prosperity sets him "in slippery places" (Ps. 73:18), as we know so well and see so clearly. "The curse of the LORD is in the house of the wicked: but he blesseth the habitation of the just" (Prov. 3:33), and it makes no difference whether house or habitation be palace or hovel.

God's doubling Job's fortunes is God's way of showing Job that in Christ he is one of God's children, for a double portion is the portion of the firstborn. God does not double his children, however, because there was no need. Job was still the parent of twenty children, dead or alive, and the ten children God gave after his trials were not a replacement for those he had so tragically lost.

They could not be replaced. It was through those last ten children that Job saw God's covenantal promise to be the God of his people and their children fulfilled. He had been faithful in God's covenant as chapter 1 tells us, and God blessed his faithfulness as he always does.

Why are Job's daughters named and not his sons? That is not an easy question to answer, but their beauty and inheritance are mentioned to emphasize once again how abundantly God restored Job's fortunes and family, giving him not only the portion of a firstborn but the most beautiful daughters in the land, who were worthy of receiving an inheritance among their brethren, though this was not ordinarily the custom in those days.

Thus ends the story of Job, not really his story, but God's. God tells us in the book of Job that he truly is the God of his people, whose love, favor, and blessing are sovereign and unchangeable. Through Christ his son he is their God—in life and in death, in prosperity and in trouble, in body and in soul. He is the God who through fire and water not only saves them but prepares them to be the richest of all who have ever lived on earth, perfect and upright, to whom none can be compared. They are his own sons and daughters for whom he will offer sacrifice until they are ready to live not in a house made with hands that can be destroyed by the winds of time, but in "an house not made with hands, eternal in the heavens" (2 Cor. 5:1), the house where Job now lives and where we will someday see him. That will not compare, though, with seeing the face of God and hearing his voice, not out of a whirlwind but in the face and voice of our savior, Jesus Christ.

JOB STUDY GUIDE

Introduction

1. Date and author:
   a. Where does scripture itself place Job in history, i.e., when did he live?
   b. Is the date of the book of Job of any importance?
   c. Do we know who the author of the book is?
2. Content:
   a. Why do some believe that the book of Job is not historical?
   b. Can you prove that the book is historical?
3. Theme and divisions:
   a. What is the main message or theme of the book?
   b. What are the main divisions of the book?

Chapters 1-2

1. Job's righteousness and wealth:
   a. Is Job's wealth mentioned because it was evidence of God's blessing?
   b. Why are Job's sacrifices for his children mentioned?
2. The first interview with Satan:
   a. What does the name *Satan* mean?
   b. Does Satan still have access to heaven?
   c. What does this passage show about the relationship between God and evil?

3. Job's trials and confession:
    a. In what way is Satan involved in the events of Job's life?
    b. What does "charged God foolishly" mean (Job 1:22)?
4. God's second interview with Satan: what is Satan's point in this second interview?
5. Job's wife: is the response of Job's wife evidence that she was unsaved?
6. Job's three friends:
    a. What was God's purpose in the visit of these three?
    b. Looking ahead, were these three friends correct in what they said to Job?
    c. Are their speeches the infallible word of God to Job?

Chapters 3-14

1. Job's first speech (chapter 3):
    a. What does it mean that Job cursed his day?
    b. Does Job sin in what he says (compare 2:10)?
    c. Are there any circumstances in which it is correct to say what Job says?
    d. What is the point of this speech, and what desire does Job express?
2. The first speeches of Eliphaz, Bildad, and Zophar (chapters 4–5; 8; 11):
    a. Of what does Eliphaz accuse Job?
    b. What does Bildad add to the accusation of Eliphaz?
    c. In what way does Zophar's speech go beyond that of the previous two?
    d. What is wrong in each of these speeches (see 32:3)?
    e. What evidence is there in their speeches that though these men sin, they are nonetheless godly men?
3. Job's replies (chapters 6–7; 9–10; 12–14):

a. What is the point of the answer of Job to each of these men?

b. Find evidence in each answer of Job's sin (see 32:2).

Chapters 15-21

1. The second speeches of Eliphaz, Bildad, and Zophar (chapters 15; 18; 20):
   a. What is the main point of each of these speeches, and what is new in relation to their previous speeches?
   b. Try to find a verse or verses in each speech that represent the theme of each.
   c. Once again find evidence in each speech of the fact that these men are sinning against Job.
   d. Is there evidence in these speeches that the three friends are having difficulty answering Job?
2. Job's continued defense (chapters 16–17; 19; 21):
   a. What point does Job make in each speech over against his three friends?
   b. Is Job in these speeches falling further into sin himself, or is he finding the right way?
   c. Why does Job speak of the resurrection in chapter 19:23–27?
3. General questions:
   a. What important biblical truths are taught in these six speeches?
   b. What details of these speeches are difficult to understand?

Chapters 22-31

1. The third speeches of Eliphaz and Bildad (chapters 22; 25):
   a. Why does Zophar not speak a third time?
   b. What is the main point of these last two speeches by Job's friends?

c. Is there evidence once again in these speeches that his friends are having difficulty answering Job?

2. Job's final defense (chapters 23–24; 26–31):
   a. Why are these last speeches of Job so lengthy?
   b. What further evidence of the triumph of Job's faith is there in these speeches?
   c. Is Job still guilty of sin in these final two speeches (see 23:11–12; 32:2)?
   d. What is the thrust of each speech?

3. General questions:
   a. Is the word *sheol* in chapter 26:6 correctly translated as *hell* or better translated as *grave* or *death*? What about chapter 24:19?
   b. Why is the reference to Adam in Job 31:33 important?

Chapters 32-37

1. The man Elihu:
   a. Why is the notice of Elihu's parentage important?
   b. Is there any reason why Elihu is not mentioned earlier?
   c. Why did Elihu wait until the others had spoken?

2. Elihu's speech:
   a. Of what sin does Elihu accuse Job's friends?
   b. Of what sin does he accuse Job?
   c. What is the main point of Elihu's speech?
   d. Does Elihu agree more with Job or with Job's friends?
   e. Is Elihu correct in what he says, or does he also err?
   f. In what respects does Elihu's speech differ from Job's last speeches?
   g. How does Elihu's speech relate to God's in the following chapters?

3. Job's lack of response:

    a. Why does Job make no response to Elihu?

    b. Find verses that indicate that Job's lack of response is more than just lack of opportunity.

Chapters 38-39

1. General questions:
   a. Why does God come to Job in a whirlwind?
   b. What is the main theme of God's speech to Job?
   c. Why does God speak of his work as creator and as the God of providence and not of his work as savior?
   d. Why is God's speech to Job in the form of questions?
   e. What do we mean when we say that God is incomprehensible?

2. Specific questions:
   a. What are some of the things mentioned in this chapter than science still does not understand?
   b. Does God emphasize more than his greatness and glory in speaking of his watchful care for his creation?
   c. What does the Belgic Confession say of the creation in article 2?
   d. What does Romans 1:18–20 say about the things that are made and what they reveal of God?
   e. Can a believer see and know God in the creation?

Chapters 40-42

1. Job's response to God:
   a. Is there a difference between what Job says in chapter 40:3–5 and chapter 42:1–6?
   b. What sin has Job repented of?
   c. What does he mean in chapter 42:5?
   d. In addition to his repentance, to what understanding and resolution of his complaints has Job come?

2. God's further revelation of himself:
   a. What or who are behemoth and leviathan?
   b. Why does God speak of these two of his works?
3. God's dealing with the three friends:
   a. What right thing had Job spoken, which God mentions in chapter 42:7–8?
   b. Why did the three friends have to ask *Job* to pray for them in addition to their offering sacrifices?
   c. Is there any significance to the seven bullocks and rams, which the three friends had to offer?
4. Job's restoration:
   a. Why did Job receive double possessions but only the same number of children?
   b. Why are the names of Job's daughters mentioned?
   c. Is there any significance to the fact that Job's restored wealth came from his relatives and acquaintances?
   d. What is the significance of the restoration of Job's earthly estate for us, and does the Lord still bless us in this way today?